Contents

D0231087

Getting the most from this book

Questions & Answers

Exam-style questions

Examiner comments on the questions
Tips on what you need to do to gain full marks, indicated by the icon ℮.

Sample student answers
Practise the questions, then look at the student answers that follow each set of questions.

Examiner commentary on sample student answers
Find out how many marks each answer would be awarded in the exam and then read the examiner comments (preceded by the icon ℮) following each student answer. Annotations that link back to points made in the student answers show exactly how and where marks are gained or lost.

AQA(A) AS Psychology

About this book

This is a guide to Unit 1 of AQA(A) AS Psychology. Unit 1 examines cognitive and developmental psychology and research methods. The guide is intended as a revision aid rather than as a textbook, and it focuses on how the specification content is examined and how different answers may be assessed.

For each of the areas, cognitive psychology, developmental psychology and research methods, the following are provided:
- The specification content for each topic, so that you know what you may be asked to demonstrate in an examination.
- Appropriate content relevant to each topic. This is not intended as the *only* appropriate content for a given topic, but gives you an idea of what you might include and how you might present an answer to a question set on a particular aspect of the specification.
- A glossary of key terms, constructed to be succinct but informative.
- Example questions in the style of AQA(A) AS examination questions, together with full explanations of their requirements as well as the appropriate breakdown of marks between AO1, AO2 and AO3 skills.
- An example grade B, C or D response to each of these questions, with examiner comments showing where marks have been gained or lost.
- An example grade A response to each of these questions, showing how the question was answered by a very strong student.

How to use this guide

This guide is *not* intended to provide a set of model answers to possible examination questions, or an account of the right material to include in any examination question. It is intended to give you an idea of how your examination will be structured and how you might improve your examination performance.

I suggest that you read through the relevant part of the Content guidance section before you attempt a question from the Question and Answer section, and that you read the suggested answers only after you have tackled the question yourself.

Content guidance

This section gives content guidance on the topics of cognitive psychology (human memory), developmental psychology (attachment) and research methods. Each topic begins with an outline of the AQA specification A requirement. This is followed by a more detailed look at the theories and studies that comprise the unit content. Knowledge of appropriate theories, studies and research methods is essential for the AS examination. It is also important to be able to assess the value of these theories, studies and research methods.

At the end of each topic, a glossary of key terms is provided — those terms that you will need to use, or may be asked to define, in an examination.

Author names and publication dates have been given when referring to research studies. The full references for these studies should be available in textbooks if you wish to research the topic further.

Cognitive psychology

Models of memory

Specification content
- *The multi-store model, including the concepts of encoding, capacity and duration. Strengths and limitations of the model*
- *The working memory model, including its strengths and limitations*

Short-term memory and long-term memory

Psychologists distinguish between **short-term memory** (STM) and **long-term memory** (LTM). STM cannot hold much information and has limited capacity, whereas LTM can hold an apparently unlimited amount of information and has a vast capacity. George Miller theorised that the capacity of STM is approximately 'seven plus or minus two' pieces of information, but that this capacity can be extended by chunking, or combining, small pieces of information. The table below shows some of the ways in which STM and LTM are different.

Comparison of short- and long-term memory

Comparison	Short-term memory (STM)	Long-term memory (LTM)
Capacity	Limited (7 ± 2 chunks)	Potentially unlimited
Duration	Short (seconds only)	Possibly lifelong
Encoding	Acoustic (sound)	Semantic (meaning)

A study of encoding in STM and LTM (Baddeley 1966)

Aims: To show that STM is largely based on acoustic code; to find out whether LTM is also acoustically encoded, and to find out whether STM or LTM is semantically encoded.

Procedures: Participants were given four sets of words to recall: (1) acoustically similar (e.g. cap, can, map); (2) acoustically dissimilar (e.g. pit, cow, pen); (3) semantically similar (e.g. big, huge, large); (4) semantically dissimilar (e.g. good, hot, safe). One group was asked to recall words immediately (from STM) and a second group was asked to recall words after a delay of 20 minutes (from LTM).

Findings: The immediate recall (STM) group remembered fewer acoustically similar than acoustically dissimilar words. The delayed recall (LTM) group showed no significant difference when remembering acoustically encoded words but differences in semantically encoded words.

Conclusions: Findings suggest acoustic encoding in STM but semantic encoding in LTM.

Criticisms: Control in laboratory experiments facilitates the identification of cause-and-effect relationships, thus the findings have high internal validity. However, laboratory experiments into memory only involve memory of facts rather than memory of experiences, thus because the findings apply only to limited aspects of memory, they have low external validity.

A study of capacity in STM (Jacobs 1987)

Aim: To research the capacity of STM.

Procedures: Participants were presented with strings of letters or digits and were asked to repeat them back in the same order. The length of the string was increased, from three to four, five, six etc., until the participant was unable to repeat the sequence accurately.

Findings: On average, participants recalled nine digits and seven letters. The average recall increased with age.

Conclusions: STM has a limited storage capacity of between five and nine items, but learned memory techniques (e.g. chunking) may increase capacity as people get older.

Criticisms: The research is artificial. In real-life settings people do not usually need to remember strings of meaningless numbers or letters, and the research therefore has low ecological validity. If the information to be remembered has more meaning, it might be remembered better.

A study of duration in LTM (Bahrick et al. 1975)

Aim: To study very long-term memories in a real-life setting.

Procedures: There were three tasks: (1) In a free recall test, 392 people were asked to list the names of their ex-classmates. (2) In a photo recognition task, participants were shown photographs of their ex-classmates and asked if they could remember the names. (3) In a name recognition task, participants were given names of their ex-classmates and asked to find the matching photographs.

Findings: Within 15 years of leaving school, participants could recognise 90% of the faces and names. Within 48 years of leaving school, participants could recognise 75% of the faces and names. Free recall memory had declined more than photo and name recognition memory.

Examiner tip
Rosy read out three random letters to Paul and asked him to repeat these, then four, five, six, seven, eight letters, and so on. When she read out ten letters, Paul could not remember them all. In an exam you could be asked to explain what Rosy was measuring.

Knowledge check 1
Outline the capacity of memory in STM.

Examiner tip

In the exam you could be asked to describe how psychologists investigate the duration of short-term memory. In your answer, include details of what the participants are asked to do and how duration of memory is measured.

Knowledge check 2

Outline two differences between STM and LTM.

Conclusions: The study shows evidence of very long-term memories in a real-life setting. Since recognition was more accurate than free recall, there may be information stored in memory that can be accessed only when we are given an appropriate cue.

Criticisms: This study was undertaken in a real-life setting and the memories were meaningful to the participants, so it has high ecological validity. It is also has application in real life: for example, carers could show elderly people photographs of their friends and colleagues in the Second World War in order to engage them in conversation.

The multi-store model of memory (Atkinson and Shiffrin 1968)

Models, or theories, of memory aim to explain how information is transferred from STM to LTM, and why sometimes it is not.

In their **multi-store model of memory**, Atkinson and Shiffrin suggest that memory comprises three separate stores: the sensory memory store, the STM and the LTM. Each store has a specific function, as shown in the diagram.

In the multi-store model, information is rehearsed in STM and, if rehearsed enough, is transferred to LTM.

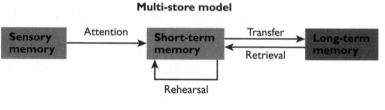

Figure 1 Multi-store model

There are three stages of information processing in the multi-store model of memory:

Stage 1: information is perceived (seen, heard etc.)

Stage 2: the information is transferred to STM, where it is maintained by rehearsal (if it is not lost or replaced by new, incoming information).

Stage 3: the information is transferred to LTM.

Examiner tip

Make sure you can draw and label a diagram of the multi-store model of memory.

Research evidence (Glanzer and Cunitz 1966)

Participants were asked to recall word lists. When words were recalled immediately, early and later words were more likely to be recalled (primacy and recency effect) due to STM and LTM effects. **Primacy effect** occurs because the first words are likely to have been transferred to LTM. **Recency effect** occurs because the last words in the list are still in STM. If there was a delay of 10 seconds or more before recall, there was only a primacy effect — only LTM was affected. This demonstrates a difference between STM and LTM.

- A strength of the multi-store model is that it is simple and can be tested. Research evidence supports the idea that STM and LTM are qualitatively different types of memory. Moreover, we have all, from time to time, 'rehearsed' information and it seems to make sense that rehearsed information is more likely to be remembered.
- However, a weakness is that, in real life, memories are created in contexts rather different from laboratory-based 'free recall' experiments, so perhaps this model does not explain fully the complexities of human memory. In addition, the model suggests that memory is a passive process, whereas theories of reconstructive memory suggest that memory is an active process.

LEV?

Knowledge check 3

Explain why the primacy and recency effects provide evidence for the multi-store model of memory.

The working memory model of memory (Baddeley and Hitch 1974)

The Baddeley and Hitch model of working memory is more complex than the multi-store model, but it focuses solely on STM or, as Baddeley and Hitch call it, **working memory**. They propose a multi-store model of STM. In their model, STM is an active processor in which the central executive 'attends to and works on' either speech-based information passed to it from the articulatory–phonological loop or visually coded information passed to it by the visual system. The three components of this model are as follows:

- The **central executive** processes information from all sensory routes; this process is 'attention-like', having limited capacity.
- The **articulatory–phonological loop** processes speech-based information. The phonological store focuses on speech perception (incoming speech) and the articulatory process focuses on speech production.
- The **visuospatial working area** (also known as the 'visuospatial scratchpad') is where spatial and visual information is processed.

Examiner tip

Make sure you can describe the three components of the working memory model.

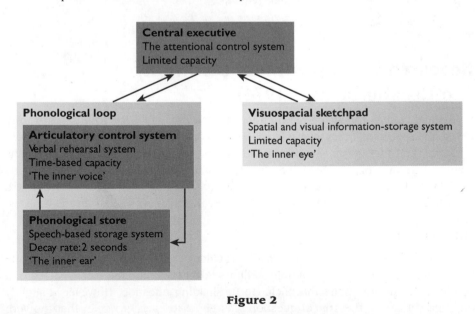

Figure 2

Examiner tip

In the exam you may need to describe the different functions of the central executive, the articulatory–phonological loop and the visuospatial working area.

Examiner tip

You should be able to refer to the working memory model to explain why a brain scan shows that, when someone is performing a verbal task, a different part of the brain is active than when performing a visual task.

Knowledge check 4

Explain how the interference task technique can be used to find evidence to support the working memory model.

The working memory model can be tested by the **interference task** technique. This technique is based on the assumption that the articulatory–phonological loop and the visuospatial scratchpad both have limited capacity to process information, so when participants are asked to perform two tasks, using the same system at the same time, their performance is affected. For instance, repeating 'the' silently while reading is difficult because both of these tasks use the articulatory–phonological loop, which has limited capacity; it cannot cope with both tasks, so the performance of one or the other will be affected.

Evaluation

Strengths
- It suggests that rehearsal is an optional process, which is more realistic than the multi-store model, especially since we do not rehearse everything that we remember.
- The model can explain how we can successfully do two tasks at the same time if the tasks involve different stores, but why we have trouble performing two tasks at the same time if the tasks involve the same stores.

Weaknesses
- Least is known about the precise function of the most important component, the central executive, and the suggestion that there may be a single central executive may be inaccurate.

Memory in everyday life

Specification content
- Eyewitness testimony (EWT). Factors affecting the accuracy of EWT, including misleading information, anxiety, age of witness
- Improving accuracy of EWT, including the use of the cognitive interview
- Strategies for memory improvement

Research into eyewitness testimony (Loftus and Palmer 1974)

Loftus and Palmer conducted research into the accuracy of **eyewitness testimony** (EWT). In Experiment 1 they investigated the effect of **leading questions** on eyewitness accounts, and in Experiment 2 they investigated the effects that leading questions have on later memory of what happened. The leading question they asked was based on 'How fast were the cars going when they smashed into each other?' but the verb 'smashed' was varied to lead participants to perceive different speeds for the vehicles.

Experiment 1

Forty-five student participants viewed a short video of a car accident. The participants were divided into five groups of nine students. After watching the video, each group was given a questionnaire that included the leading question. However, a slightly different version of the critical question was given to each group, in that the verb varied between 'smashed', 'collided', 'bumped', 'hit' and 'contacted'. As shown in the bar chart, the leading question affected the participants' perception of speed. The conclusion was that the way questions are worded may affect perception and recall.

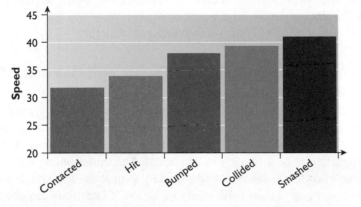

Figure 3 Experiment 1: estimated speed for verb used

Experiment 2

One hundred and fifty student participants (three groups of 50) viewed a short video of a car accident. Afterwards they were given a questionnaire. Again, the critical leading question was based on 'How fast were the cars going when they smashed into each other?' However, group 1 was asked the critical question containing the word 'hit', group 2 was asked it with the word 'smashed' and group 3 (the control group) was not asked the leading question.

A week later, the participants were asked to return and answer more questions, including 'Did you see any broken glass?' (there was no broken glass in the film clip). The findings are shown in the bar chart. Those participants who thought the car was travelling faster (the 'smashed' group) were more likely to report seeing broken glass. This suggests that their memory of a car travelling faster led them to 'invent' a memory in line with this expectation.

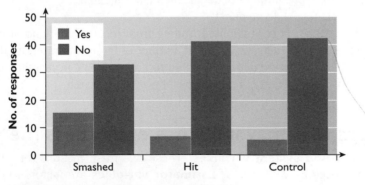

Figure 4 Experiment 2: response to 'Did you see any broken glass?'

The findings from these two experiments suggest that leading questions do have an effect on what eyewitnesses think they have seen.

Criticism: There is some evidence from real-life studies that recall is not affected by leading questions — perhaps because emotional arousal makes the original image stronger. However, the high levels of control in the laboratory experiment meant that it was possible to show clearly that EWT could be affected by the way questions were asked. The results have a useful application in real life — when the testimony of an eyewitness could lead to a person being convicted of a crime.

Eyewitness memory of a crime (Yuille and Cutshall 1986)

Aim: To examine eyewitness accounts of a real event.

Sample: 21 witnesses to a gun-shooting crime were interviewed by police. Four to five months after the incident, 20 witnesses were contacted and 13 agreed to be re-interviewed; 10 were male and 3 female and their ages ranged from 15 to 32.

Method: Case study of a real event (shooting). The initial police interviews were made available to the researchers and included a verbatim account of the event in the witness's words and their responses to a series of questions designed to clarify aspects of the event.

Research interviews were conducted 4–5 months after the event at a time and place chosen by the witness. Interviews were between 45 and 90 minutes long and followed the same procedures as the police interview: an account in the witness's own words followed by questions to clarify earlier points and solicit specific details. The questions included two misleading ones. One misleading question asked about a broken headlight: 6 of the witnesses were asked if they had seen 'the busted headlight' and the remainder were asked if they had seen 'a busted headlight' (there was no broken headlight). Another similar question was asked about a differently coloured panel on the car. These questions were chosen because, although the car was in full view of all the witnesses, the car did not play a major part in the event.

Scoring: The event was reconstructed from police evidence (photographs, confiscated weapons, witness descriptions etc.) and reports of other professionals attending the scene (ambulance men etc). Each detail recalled was awarded 1 point.

Results: The research interview elicited considerably more detail than the police interview:

- Police interview: number of details recalled   649.5
- Research interview: number of details recalled   1,056.5

Misleading questions had no effect.

Conclusion: This is a very different finding from most of the laboratory research conducted into EWT. There was a small amount of information reported that never happened (2.93% of action details reported to police, 3.23% in research interviews), but this is lower than is often reported by laboratory research.

Knowledge check 5

Outline two differences between the research by Loftus and Palmer and the Yuille and Cutshall research.

Factors that may influence eyewitness memory

- **Estimator and system variables.** These two main reasons for witness error were proposed by Wells (1978). **Estimator variables** are factors to do with the witness. They might include levels of stress and whether or not the criminal was carrying a weapon. **System variables** are factors where the justice system has some control, such as preventing the use of leading questions (e.g. Loftus and Palmer 1974).

- **Duration of event and time of day.** The longer we watch, the more likely we are to remember details. Witnesses also remember more when they see something during the day or at night, but twilight is not very good. It seems that people make more effort when it is dark because they know that viewing conditions are poor.
- **Violence distraction.** People have a better memory for non-violent events. Clifford and Scott (1978) showed their participants two short films, one violent and one not, and participants remembered more about the non-violent film.
- **The amount of time between an event and recall.** This will influence memory — the longer the time, the worse the recall. This is known as **trace-dependent forgetting**. Over time, the memory trace will disappear because when memory circuits are not activated for long periods, the connections between them may weaken to the point where the circuit is broken and the information is lost.
- **Emotion (stress).** Highly emotional events may be either more memorable or less memorable than everyday events. **Flashbulb memories** can be described as memories of emotional events that last for a lifetime. Christianson and Hubinette (1993) found that emotional involvement does increase the accuracy of memory. They interviewed 110 people who had witnessed a bank robbery. Witnesses who had been personally threatened during the crime, and who were more emotionally involved, had more accurate memories than the witnesses who said they were not very involved. However, Freud suggested that **repression** is the way we protect our ego (conscious mind) from unpleasant memories, and that unhappy or traumatic memories are more likely to be forgotten because we are unconsciously motivated to forget events that make us uncomfortable.
- **Age of a witness.** Some research suggests that age affects how well people remember events. Cohen and Faulkner (1989) showed two groups of participants a film of a kidnapping. The average age of one group of participants was 70. The average age of the second group of participants was 35. Both groups were asked leading questions when were questioned about the film. The older participants were significantly more likely to be misled by the leading questions.

Examiner tip
You may find it helpful to make a chart identifying the factors that influence eyewitness memory and why these factors affect memory.

Improving the reliability of eyewitness testimony

The cognitive interview (Geiselman 1985)

The **cognitive interview** is a procedure used by the police to help eyewitnesses recall information more accurately. During the interview the witness is encouraged to:
- report every detail, no matter how seemingly trivial
- recreate the context of the event
- recall the event in different orders (in reverse, partially etc.)
- recall the event from other perspectives (imagining what someone in a different place may have seen)

While the interview is progressing, the police take care to:
- reduce the anxiety felt by witnesses
- minimise any distractions
- allow the witness to take his or her time
- avoid interruptions and leading questions

This type of interview has been found to achieve up to 35% improvement in the accuracy of recall, especially if the interview takes place shortly after the event.

Knowledge check 6

Outline how a cognitive interview is used to investigate memory of an event, including *at least one* example of what a participant would be asked to do.

Strategies for memory improvement

Levels of processing theory (Craik and Lockhart 1972)

Craik and Lockhart theorise that whether or not we remember information depends on how it is processed. They describe three levels of processing:

- **iconic** — what information looks like (e.g. daughter)
- **acoustic** — what information sounds like ('doorter')
- **semantic** — what information means (female offspring)

In terms of levels of processing, iconic processing is shallow, acoustic processing is deeper and semantic processing is the deepest. Information that is processed deeply will be remembered better than shallowly processed information.

Examiner tip

Make sure you can apply the Craik and Lockhart research to suggest a strategy for memory improvement.

Based on Craik and Lockhart, one effective technique is known as **elaborative rehearsal**. An example of this might be to read the definition of a key term, study the definition of that term, and then read a more detailed description of what that term means. After repeating this process a few times, your recall of the information will be far better. Moreover, if you explain new concepts to others, this enhances your understanding and recall, so try to teach a friend what you are learning.

The organisation of memory (Collins and Quillian 1969)

Collins and Quillian proposed that concepts are stored hierarchically in our 'mental dictionary'. Relationships between concepts are represented within the hierarchy: for example, the concept of 'animal' would be stored at a node that is above 'bird', which would be stored above 'canary'. Connected to each category node are properties, such as 'has skin' and 'can move around' for 'animal'. Collins and Quillian predicted that the more closely situated on the hierarchy the concepts were, the faster they would activate each other: that is, people should be faster to say that the proposition 'Birds have feathers' is true than to say that 'Birds eat' is true.

If Collins and Quillian are correct, then when information is organised into clusters it is more likely to be remembered because each remembered concept will activate other related information. You can take advantage of this by grouping similar concepts and terms together, or make an outline of your notes and textbook readings to help group related concepts. Also by thinking about and establishing relationships between new ideas and previously existing memories, you can increase the likelihood of recalling the recently learned information.

Mnemonics

A **mnemonic** is a memory aid, often verbal, and sometimes in verse form, which can be used to remember lists. One common mnemonic device is to use an easily remembered word, phrase or rhyme, whose initials or other characteristics are associated with the list items. For instance, to remember the order of the colours in the spectrum (red, orange, yellow, green, blue, indigo, violet), 'Richard Of York Gave Battle In Vain' is popular. A mnemonic for approximating the digits of pi is 'May I have a large container of coffee?' because counting the letters in each word yields the sequence 3, 1, 4, 1, 5, 9, 2, 6.

Memory: glossary of terms

capacity: a measure of how much information can be stored in STM and LTM. Capacity of STM is thought to be 7 ± 2 chunks of information. LTM is thought to have unlimited capacity for many types of information.

cognitive interview: a procedure used by the police to help eyewitnesses recall information more accurately. During the interview the witness is encouraged to relax and recall everything they can remember, no matter how trivial the information appears. During recall the police do not ask questions or interrupt the witness.

duration: a measure of how long information is held in memory. In STM the duration of information, if not rehearsed, is very short — less than 30 seconds. In LTM the duration of information may be a lifetime.

encoding: the form in which information is stored in memory. In STM information is thought to be stored in acoustic code (by sound). In LTM information is thought to be stored in semantic code (by meaning).

eyewitness testimony (EWT): descriptions of events given by people who were present at the time (e.g. in criminal trials). Eyewitness descriptions may include descriptions of people, places, sequences of events and other information.

flashbulb memory: an accurate and long-lasting memory of the details of the context of an event created at a time of intense emotion — as if a flash photograph has been taken where every detail is printed in memory.

leading question: a question that suggests a certain kind of answer. For example, 'Was the burglar's hat black or brown?' suggests that the burglar was wearing a hat.

Knowledge check 7

Sophie made a list of the facts she needed to learn for her psychology exam. Jane also made a list but organised her facts into categories such as multi-store model of memory, working memory model, strategies for memory improvement. Explain why organising facts into categories may help Jane remember more in the exam.

Examiner tip

It might be useful in the exam if you can explain what a mnemonic is, and give an example.

levels of processing: the suggestion that the duration of a memory is dependent on the way that information is processed, and that if information is processed deeply (e.g. organised or elaborated in some way), it will be remembered for longer.

long-term memory (LTM): relatively permanent memory that has unlimited capacity and duration.

memory: the process by which we retain information, including encoding, storage and retrieval of experiences.

mnemonic: a memory aid that can be used to remember lists (e.g. one is a bun, two is a shoe, three is a tree etc.).

multi-store model of memory: the model of memory which proposes that information enters our mind through sensory perception, which is then passed to a short-term store (STM) where it is held for a brief duration unless rehearsed. Rehearsal leads to transfer to long-term store (LTM).

reconstructive memory: an explanation of how we store and remember long-term memories in terms of social and cultural processes, which explains why both the creation of a memory and later recall may be distorted by schemas and stereotypes.

repression: a method of keeping anxiety-provoking information out of conscious awareness — called 'motivated forgetting'. Freud proposed that repression is an ego-defence mechanism and that repressed information may surface in dreams or in Freudian slips.

short-term memory (STM): a temporary store for information which is limited in capacity (7 ± 2 chunks of information) and duration (probably less than 30 seconds). Information in STM is thought to be stored acoustically (by sounds) rather than semantically (by meaning).

working memory model: a model of STM which suggests that one area of memory processes the information we are currently working on. This information is processed by a phonological loop (acoustic data) and/or by a visuospatial scratchpad (visual data). Both the phonological loop and the visuospatial scratchpad are organised by a central executive.

Knowledge summary

You should be able to:

- describe and evaluate the multi-store model of memory
- explain the concepts of memory encoding, capacity and duration
- describe and evaluate the working memory model
- differentiate between the multi-store model of memory and the working memory model
- define what is meant by eyewitness memory
- describe and evaluate research into eyewitness memory

- identify factors affecting the accuracy of EWT
- explain how misleading information, anxiety, and the age of a witness can affect EWT
- describe psychological research into improving accuracy of EWT
- describe the procedures involved in a cognitive interview and explain why the cognitive interview should increase the accuracy of witness recall
- suggest, describe and apply strategies for memory improvement — and explain why these may improve the ability to recall information memory

Developmental psychology

Attachment

Specification content

- *Explanations of attachment, including learning theory and Bowlby's theory*
- *Types of attachment: secure attachment, insecure-avoidant and insecure-resistant*
- *Use of the 'strange situation' in attachment research*
- *Cultural variations in attachment*
- *The effects of disruption of attachment, failure to form attachment (privation) and institutional care*

Developmental psychologists study the changes that occur as people grow from childhood, through adolescence, and into adulthood. **Attachments**, which are strong emotional bonds that form as a result of interaction between two people, occur throughout our life span. Schaffer (1993) defines attachment as 'a close emotional relationship between two persons characterised by mutual affection and a desire to maintain closeness'.

Explanations of attachment

Why do infants develop attachments? Explanations of attachments try to account for how and why children become attached to a caregiver. This account focuses on two theories of attachment: the learning theory explanation (behavioural); and Bowlby's theory of attachment.

The behavioural explanation (learning theory)

The basic principle of learning theory is that all behaviour is learned. The main argument proposed by behavioural theorists is that the infant's emotional dependence on, and bond with, his or her caregiver can be explained in terms of reinforcement arising from the satisfaction of basic physiological needs, such as food and drink. The mother (or caregiver) relieves these needs and thus acquires reward value as the infant learns to associate pleasure with the caregiver.

Based on **classical conditioning**, receiving food gives the infant pleasure, so when the caregiver feeds him or her, the infant feels pleasure. Thus an association is formed between the caregiver and food, so that whenever the caregiver is near, the infant feels pleasure — expressed as attachment behaviour.

Based on **operant conditioning**, infants feel discomfort when they are hungry and so desire food to remove the discomfort. They learn that if they cry, their caregiver feeds them and the discomfort is removed. This is **negative reinforcement**: the consequences of behaviour (crying) lead to something unpleasant ceasing (feeling hungry stops). Thus, proximity-seeking behaviour is reinforced, which in turn leads to the attachment behaviour of distress on being separated from the caregiver.

Examiner tip

Make sure you can write a definition for the term **attachment**.

Knowledge check 8

Outline how behaviourist psychologists explain attachment.

Evaluation

- Feeding cannot fully explain the development of attachments. Harlow (1959) placed young monkeys with two 'mothers'. One was a wire 'mother' with a feeding bottle attached and the other 'mother' was covered in cloth but had no feeding bottle. The monkeys showed a preference for the cloth-covered mother, especially when they were distressed. This shows that attachment is not just about food. Harlow also found that, as adults, these monkeys found it difficult to form reproductive relationships and were poor mothers. This suggests that the lack of interaction with a caregiver may cause later maladjustment.

Bowlby's theory of attachment (1969)

Bowlby suggested that social behaviours, such as following, clinging, sucking, smiling and crying, are innate, and that the function of this behaviour is to bond the child to its caregiver. Bowlby suggested that infants are born with an innate drive to form attachments and that infants possess characteristics (**social releasers**, such as smiles) that facilitate the caregiver's attachment to them. According to Bowlby, attachment is an **interactive and innate two-way relationship**, in which the caregiver is as attached as the infant. The role of attachment is adaptive, as it promotes survival by (a) maintaining proximity (closeness) between infant and caregiver; (b) assisting cognitive development; and (c) providing the opportunity for learning through imitation.

Bowlby proposed that infants have many attachments but that the one at the top of the hierarchy has special significance for emotional development. The infant becomes most closely attached to the individual who responds in the most sensitive manner, which leads the infant to have one primary attachment object (**monotropy**). The primary attachment object need not be the infant's biological mother. The child learns from the relationship with the primary caregiver and this relationship acts as a **template** for future relationships. Bowlby called this an **internal working model** (a cognitive schema) that generates expectations for all future relationships.

Bowlby's attachment theory focuses on the interpersonal processes that create attachments, particularly the innate tendency in infants to seek attachment and to elicit caregiver responses through smiles and other social releasers. Bowlby proposed that the development of attachments follows an innate maturational sequence.

Examiner tip

Make sure you can explain why attachment is adaptive behaviour.

Phase 1: birth to 8 weeks

- Orientation and signals are directed towards people without discrimination.
- Infants behave in characteristic and friendly ways towards other people, but their ability to discriminate between them is limited.

Phase 2: 8–10 weeks to 6 months

- Orientation and signals are directed towards one or more special people.
- Infants continue to be generally friendly, but there is beginning to be a difference of behaviour towards one primary caregiver.

Phase 3: 6 months to 1–2 years old

- There is maintenance of closeness to a special person by means of locomotion as well as signals.
- The infant starts to follow his or her caregiver (displaying **separation anxiety**), greets the caregiver when he or she returns, and uses the caregiver as a safe base from which to explore.
- The infant selects other people as subsidiary attachment figures but treats strangers with caution (**stranger anxiety**).

Bowlby proposed that attachment between human infants and their caregivers is **adaptive behaviour** (evolutionary explanation). He suggested that there is a sensitive period that ends at around 1–3 years, during which infants develop a special attachment to one individual.

Factors that influence the development of attachments

Attachments are influenced by the following factors:

- **The age of the child.** Bowlby proposed that unless attachments have developed by between 1 and 3 years, they will not develop 'normally'.
- **The child's temperament.** Some aspects of temperament may be innate and a child's temperament may make it easier or harder for him or her to form attachments.
- **The quality of care.** Psychologists suggest that the sensitivity of the caregiver can also affect the development of attachments. Ainsworth et al. (1974) proposed that good, secure attachment is promoted by sensitive responsiveness from a caregiver and that attachment is related to the quality of the interactions between the infant and his or her caregiver. In support of this theory, Isabella et al. (1989) found that responsiveness in the mother towards a 1-month-old baby correlated with a close relationship between mother and baby at 1 year.

Types of attachment

There are individual and cultural differences in styles of attachment. For example, some infants are **securely attached** whereas others are **insecurely attached**. Ainsworth and Bell (1970) developed the **strange situation** procedures to measure differences in infant attachment.

The strange situation (Ainsworth and Bell 1970)

The strange situation procedures involve controlled observation that allows researchers to assess how securely an infant is attached to a caregiver. It comprises seven episodes, each lasting about 3 minutes:

(1) The caregiver carries the infant into a room, puts the infant on the floor and then sits in a chair and does not interact with the infant unless the infant seeks attention.
(2) A stranger enters the room and talks with the caregiver, then approaches the infant with a toy.

Knowledge check 9

Why is Bowlby's theory of attachment a 'nature' rather than a 'nurture' theory of attachment?

(3) The caregiver leaves. If the infant plays, the stranger observes unobtrusively. If the infant is passive, the stranger tries to interest him or her in a toy. If the infant shows distress (crying), the stranger tries to comfort him or her.

(4) The caregiver returns and the stranger leaves.

(5) After the infant begins to play, the caregiver leaves and the infant is briefly left alone.

(6) The stranger re-enters the room and repeats the behaviour as described in step 3 above.

(7) The caregiver returns and the stranger leaves.

The strange situation procedure places the infant in a mildly stressful situation in order to observe four types of behaviour:

- **separation anxiety** — a securely attached child shows some anxiety but is fairly easily soothed
- **willingness to explore** — a securely attached child explores more when the caregiver is present
- **stranger anxiety** — the degree of security of attachment is related to the degree of stranger anxiety
- **reunion behaviour** — an insecurely attached infant may ignore the caregiver's return

Examiner tip
You should be able to describe the procedure used in the strange situation and the four types of behaviour that are observed.

Three attachment types

Secure attachment. Securely attached infants show some anxiety when their caregiver departs but are easily soothed and greet the caregiver's return with enthusiasm. These infants play independently and return to the caregiver regularly for reassurance. Ainsworth et al. concluded that a secure attachment is associated with sensitivity in the caregiver, which teaches the infant to expect the same in other relationships. Secure attachment is generally related to healthy cognitive and emotional development, involving independence, self-confidence and trusting relationships.

Insecure–avoidant attachment. The infant shows indifference when the caregiver leaves, and does not display stranger anxiety. At reunion the infant actively avoids contact with the caregiver. The caregiver tends to be insensitive and may ignore the infant during play. These infants play independently.

Insecure–resistant attachment. The infant is distressed when the caregiver goes and, although when the caregiver returns he or she rushes to the caregiver, the infant is not easily consoled. The infant may resist contact with the caregiver, or may seek comfort and reject it at the same time. These children explore less than other children. In samples of middle-class American children, Ainsworth et al. found that about 65% were classed as secure, 15% were classed as insecure–avoidant and 20% insecure–resistant.

Knowledge check 10
Briefly describe how the behaviour of a securely attached infant differs from that of an insecurely attached infant.

Main and Solomon (1986) added a fourth type of attachment — **disorganised attachment** — in which there are no set patterns of behaviour at separation or reunion.

How reliable is the strange situation?

Main et al. (1985) conducted a longitudinal study. Infants were assessed in the strange situation before the age of 18 months with both their mothers and fathers. When the children were retested at the age of 6 years, the researchers found considerable consistency in security of attachment to both parents. Of the secure babies, 100% were classified as securely attached to both parents at 6 years, and 75% of avoidant babies were reclassified as avoidant at age 6.

Cultural variation in the development of attachment

If infant attachment is innate, then attachment behaviour should be similar in all cultures.

Sagi, van Ijzendoorn and Koren-Karie (1991) studied attachment styles of infants in the USA, Israel, Japan and Germany. They reported as follows:

* **American children** — 71% secure attachment, 12% insecure–resistant, 17% insecure–avoidant.
* **Israeli children** (raised in a kibbutz) — 62% secure attachment, 33% insecure–resistant, 5% insecure–avoidant. The children in the kibbutz were looked after by adults who were not their family, but they saw few strangers. This may explain why the children were not anxious when their caregiver left but were anxious when the stranger appeared.
* **Japanese children** — 68% secure attachment, 32% insecure–resistant and few insecure–avoidant. It was noted that Japanese children are rarely left by their mother, so the mother leaving during the strange situation may have been particularly stressful. Their anxious behaviour may be the result of the mother leaving rather than of a stranger arriving.
* **German children** — 40% securely attached, 49% insecure–avoidant, 11% insecure–resistant. German children are encouraged to be independent and not to be 'clingy'. The high percentage of insecure–avoidant children may reflect the cultural ethos of valuing independence.

Analysis of strange situation studies (van Ijzendoorn and Kroonenberg 1988)

The researchers compared the results of 32 strange situation studies in eight countries (involving 2,000 children).

Country	Number of studies	Percentage of each attachment type		
		Secure	Avoidant	Resistant
West Germany	3	57	35	8
Great Britain	1	75	22	3
Netherlands	4	67	26	7
Sweden	1	74	22	4
Israel	2	64	7	29
Japan	2	68	5	27
China	1	50	25	25
USA	18	65	21	14
Average		**65**	**20**	**14**

Criticisms: Variations within one culture were 1.5 times greater than variations between cultures, which suggests that any one culture may comprise several subcultures. Although large numbers of children were studied overall, some sample sizes were small. In the Chinese study, for example, only 36 children were used and it may be unsafe to generalise the results to all Chinese infants as 36 children may not be representative of the population. The strange situation is based on US culture and observed behaviour may not have the same meaning in different cultures. The use of procedures developed in one culture may not be a valid measure of behaviour in another culture.

Disruption of attachment

In developmental psychology:

- **Separation** is when a child is separated from his or her attachment figure for a relatively short period of time.
- **Deprivation** is the loss of something that is needed. Maternal deprivation occurs when a child has formed an attachment but then experiences the loss of the mother or other attachment figure. The loss is long term or permanent and the attachment bond is broken.
- **Privation** means never having been able to satisfy a certain need. Maternal privation is when a child has never been able to form a close relationship (develop an attachment) with any one caregiver.

Separation: the protest, despair, detachment (PDD) model

Bowlby (1952) and Robertson and Robertson (1968) studied young children who were separated from their attachment figure (usually their mother). The researchers found there were three stages in the children's separation behaviours:

Stage 1: protest. During this stage, the child protests at the separation by crying (which may be continuous), calling for his or her mother or caregiver and showing signs of panic.

Stage 2: despair. After a day or so, the child appears to lose interest in his or her surroundings, becomes withdrawn, cries less frequently and may eat and sleep poorly.

Stage 3: detachment. The child cries less and appears to have recovered, becoming more alert and interested in his or her surroundings. If the caregiver reappears, the child may not show much interest. The attachment bond between the child and the caregiver may be damaged, but most children re-establish their attachment to the caregiver over time. For some, however, the bond may be permanently broken.

Evidence for the PDD model (Robertson and Robertson 1968)

James and Joyce Robertson observed and filmed the responses of healthy young children to separation from their mothers or caregivers. Their intention was to show that the distress experienced by some children when separated could be reduced or even prevented if they were given substitute emotional care. They observed the behaviour of five children, aged 1–2, whose mothers were hospitalised for between 9 and 27 days for the birth of a new baby. The results for two of the children were as follows.

John: 17 months (9 days in a residential nursery)

In the nursery, the system of group care made it impossible for John to find a substitute mother. The nurses did not understand or respond to his attention-seeking behaviour. Under the cumulative stress of separation from his mother, the lack of 'mothering' from the nurses, the strange food and institutional routines, eventually he refused food and drink, stopped playing, cried a great deal and gave up trying to get the nurses' attention. Visits from his father failed to relieve his anxiety. Upon reunion with his mother, John screamed and struggled when she tried to hold him.

Jane: 17 months (10 days in foster care)

Jane was placed in a foster home (the Robertson family home) for 10 days. Food and routines were kept similar to those at home, her father visited her daily and the foster mother was fully available to meet Jane's needs. After the first few days she showed the strain of separation by increased sucking, impatience and resistance to being handled, but she slept and ate well and related warmly to the foster family. Supportive care prevented excessive anxiety, and although she was reluctant to give up the foster mother, Jane's reunion with her natural mother was not difficult.

The Robertsons concluded that:
- the short-term separation had serious effects on John, including possible permanent damage to his attachment to his mother
- the child's ability to cope with separation from the mother is affected by age, the level of maturity, the parent–child relationship and the quality of substitute care.

Maternal deprivation: Bowlby's maternal deprivation hypothesis

Bowlby (1953) proposed that long-term maternal deprivation — the loss of the mother figure or other attachment figure — is harmful: 'Mother love in infancy and childhood is as important for mental health as are vitamins and proteins for physical health' (Bowlby, 1951).

Bowlby suggested that continuous 'maternal care' is necessary for emotional and cognitive development (maternal care may be provided by a 'mother substitute'). This is a 'critical period' hypothesis because, according to Bowlby, there is a critical period, before the age of 2½, during which maternal deprivation will affect development and the effects will be permanent.

In sum, deprivation of the primary caregiver during the critical period has harmful effects on the child's emotional, social and cognitive development. The long-term effects may include separation anxiety expressed as 'clingy behaviour' and reluctance to attend school, and future relationships may be affected by emotional insecurity.

Maternal privation

Maternal privation is when a child has never been able to develop an attachment to his or her mother or another caregiver.

Rutter (1981) argued that the term 'maternal deprivation' is misleading because 'deprivation' refers to a variety of different experiences and outcomes. He also argued that even when separation is related to psychosocial problems, this does not mean that separation causes poor development, and that affectionless psychopathy may be the result of an initial failure to develop attachments, rather than a result of broken attachments. This is the distinction between privation (a lack of attachments) and deprivation (a loss of attachments).

Examiner tip
Make sure you know the difference between separation, deprivation and privation.

Case studies of maternal privation

Genie: Curtiss (1989)

Genie was discovered at the age of 13. She had been kept in one room, isolated, beaten and malnourished. Although she was given extensive education, and her perceptual skills were reported to be near normal, her language skills did not develop normally. As she grew up, she had a series of difficult relationships with carers.

The Koluchova twins (Koluchova 1976, 1991)

The researcher studied twin boys who had been locked in a cellar and who had suffered extreme privation until the age of 7. When found, the children had virtually no language skills. When they were 9, they were fostered in a loving home. By the age of 14 their behaviour and intellect were normal. By the age of 20 they were described as of above average intelligence and having loving relationships with members of their foster family.

The concentration camp children (Freud and Dann 1951)

The researchers studied six orphans who had spent their first 3 years, without continuous adult care, in a concentration camp. They were strongly attached to each other and were afraid of being separated. At first they were hostile towards adults, but eventually they developed normal social and cognitive skills. As adults they were described as being within the 'normal range' of development.

Evaluation points from these case studies

Although these are all case studies, which makes it impossible to generalise, the differences between the cases are important. The following factors should be considered:

- duration of privation (Genie's was the longest)
- experiences during privation (the Koluchova twins had each other for company, as did the concentration camp children; Genie also suffered physical, social and emotional abuse, was alone and was not placed in a loving foster home)
- quality of care following privation (the twins were adopted but Genie was passed between academic psychologists as a research interest and then placed in an institution)
- individual differences in the temperament and intellect of the child

Examiner tip
You need to be able to explain the advantages and limitations of the case study method.

A key study on maternal privation: Hodges and Tizard (1989)

Hodges and Tizard (1989) looked at whether there is a critical (or sensitive) period in which failure to make a secure attachment can be shown to affect adult relationships. They studied a group of children from their early days in an institution (children's home) until they were 16 years old. Some of the children were adopted and experienced 'normal' emotional attachments. This enabled the researchers to observe whether early privation was associated with long-term emotional damage.

Sixty-five children were studied. The children had been placed in an institution before they were 4 months old. The 'home' had a policy against the 'caretakers' forming attachments to the children and, before the age of 4, the children had had an average of 50 different caretakers. Thus the children (and caretakers) were unlikely to have formed any specific attachments.

By the age of 4, 24 of the institutionalised children had been adopted, 15 had returned to their natural homes (the 'restored' group) and the rest remained in the institution. The children were assessed then, and again when they were 8 years old, at which time the sample was reduced to 51 children.

By the time the children reached the age of 16, the researchers were able to locate and interview 23 of the adopted children (some of whom had been adopted after the age of 4), 11 'restored' children and 5 children who had remained in institutions. A comparison (control) group, consisting of children matched for age and gender with the children in the sample, was established.

The emotional adjustment of the children was assessed using interviews and questionnaires conducted with the children, their matched controls, their parents or caretakers and their teachers. The data collected concerned attitudes and behaviour.

> **Knowledge check 11**
> Define maternal privation.

Findings at age 16 were as follows:

- **Relationships within the family.** The adopted children were as closely attached to their parents as the comparison group, whereas the restored group was much less likely to be closely attached. Restored children were reportedly less cuddly, harder to give affection to, and less involved with their families.
- **Peer relationships.** All the ex-institution adolescents were less likely to have a special friend, to be part of a crowd or to be liked by other children. They were more quarrelsome and more likely to be bullies.
- **Other adults outside the family.** The ex-institution children were more attention seeking and the restored children were more aggressive.
- **Summary.** The comparison and adopted children were most similar in terms of relationships within the family. In relationships with peers and with adults outside the family, the adopted and restored ex-institution children were most similar.

Five possible explanations can be offered for the results:

- The adopted families were more middle class than the restored families — was there a class-related difference?
- Perhaps the adopted children suffered from poor self-esteem because they were adopted, which affected their relationships outside the home.

Examiner tip

Can you explain why the study by Hodges and Tizard is a study of maternal privation?

Knowledge check 12

Hodges and Tizard found that the adopted children formed good relationships with their families but not with their peers. Give one explanation for this finding.

- Adoptive parents put a lot of effort into relationships between themselves and their children but not between the children and their peers. This would explain why the adopted children had good relationships with parents but not with their peers. Restored children had no special help with any relationships, which explains why they had difficulty in all relationships.
- Perhaps the ability to form peer relationships is especially affected by early emotional deprivation. Therefore, the adopted children were able to recover their family relationships when given good emotional care, but the same did not happen for their peer relationships.
- Perhaps the ex-institutional children lag behind their peers in emotional development.

Attachment in everyday life

Specification content

- *The impact of different forms of daycare on children's social development, including the effects on aggression and peer relations*
- *How research into attachment and daycare has influenced childcare practices*

Daycare and social development

Psychologists are interested in whether daycare has a positive or negative effect on social and cognitive development. **Daycare** refers to temporary care for a child provided by someone other than his or her parents (excluding school). Daycare can be provided in a variety of ways, usually not in the child's home, by nurseries, childminders or nannies, but does not include residential care or fostering.

The debate surrounding daycare focuses on three issues:
- **Is daycare harmful?** In 1951, the World Health Organization (WHO) stated that day nurseries would cause permanent damage to the emotional health of a future generation. They based this conclusion on Bowlby's theory of maternal deprivation.
- **Is daycare beneficial?** In the USA in the 1960s, daycare schemes were established to improve pre-school opportunities for disadvantaged children. The best-known scheme was a programme called 'Headstart', which was supposed to benefit poor children so that they could start school having equal opportunities with their peers.
- **Double standards?** Kagan et al. (1980) suggested that a double standard was being applied, where daycare was considered good for 'lower-class' children in that it improved their cognitive ability, but not for middle-class children because of the effect of maternal deprivation.

Research into daycare

Headstart (USA) was a pre-school enrichment programme intended to improve the opportunities of disadvantaged children. Research found that those who had attended enrichment programmes (in day nurseries) had more advanced cognitive skills than 'unenriched' children from similar backgrounds, but that by the age of 11 these differences had disappeared. In adolescence, fewer Headstart children were on welfare, more were in college and fewer were delinquent.

This programme was large and varied, so it is difficult to evaluate, but there did not seem to be any negative effects of intensive pre-school education.

Kagan et al. (1980) set up their own nursery school in Boston (USA), where they studied the effects of nursery care. Close emotional contact was ensured because each member of staff had responsibility for only a small group of children.

The study looked at 33 infants who had attended the nursery full time from the age of 3½ months and compared them with a matched control group of children who stayed at home. The children were assessed for 2½ years on attachment, cognitive ability and sociability. No significant differences were found between the groups, but there was a wide range of individual differences unrelated to the form of care. It was concluded that daycare was not harmful.

Research into childminding

Childminding is a form of daycare that some suggest should be preferable to day nurseries because it is closer to home care, but research does not always support this assertion.

Mayall and Petrie (1983) studied childminders in London. The study involved a group of children under the age of 2 and their mothers and childminders. The study found that the quality of care varied; some childminders were excellent, but others provided an unstimulating environment in which the children in their care failed to thrive. There was no control group, however; it is thus possible that some children cared for at home are equally unstimulated.

Bryant et al. (1980) studied childminders in a middle-class area in Oxfordshire. Seventy-five per cent of the children were described as passive and detached and 25% as disturbed and having poor language skills. Many minders were untrained and rewarded the children for quiet and passive behaviour. Bryant suggested that many minders do not see it as part of their job to form emotional bonds with the children or to stimulate them.

Effects of daycare on social development

Does daycare harm social development by damaging attachment bonds? Some research shows a negative effect, some a positive effect and some no effect. Many factors may influence how daycare affects a child, including the quality of care, the child's temperament and his or her home background.

The negative effects of daycare (Belsky and Rovine 1988)

Two groups of children were selected. One group had experienced no daycare and the other had experienced at least 20 hours' daycare each week before their first birthday. The children were placed in the 'strange situation' to test how strong their attachments were.

Examiner tip
Most research into the effects of daycare is correlational research. You must be able to explain the advantages and disadvantages of using correlational research to measure the effects of daycare.

Knowledge check 13
A researcher asked 50 mothers to record the amount of time their child spent in daycare and to rate their children for aggressiveness. As the amount of time spent in daycare increased, the mother's rating of aggression also increased. Explain what kind of correlation this research showed.

The children who had been in daycare were said to have insecure attachment types, either insecure–avoidant (they ignored their mothers and did not mind when the mothers left) or insecure–resistant (they were unsettled when their mothers were present but upset when the mothers left). Those who had not experienced daycare were more likely to be securely attached. It was concluded that daycare has a negative effect on social development.

The positive effects of daycare (Shea 1981)

Two groups of children were selected. Both were aged between 3 and 4. One group attended nursery school for 5 days each week and the other group attended just twice each week. During their first 10 weeks of attending nursery school, the children were assessed for their social skills. Both groups increased their social skills, were less aggressive and interacted more with others. The social skills of the 5-days-a-week group improved more rapidly. It was concluded that daycare has a positive effect on social development.

Implications for childcare practices

Many factors may impact on whether daycare has positive or negative effects on cognitive development: how well the staff are trained; the ratio of staff to children; minimal staff turnover to facilitate stable attachments with carers; and appropriate toys and activities.

According to McCartney (2004), whether daycare poses a risk to children, protects them from disadvantaged homes, or promotes good developmental outcomes, depends on the **quality of care**. Evidence suggests that individual characteristics, such as temperament, cognitive ability and gender, influence how children experience daycare. In most studies, family variables are better predictors of children's development than are daycare variables. Quality daycare may buffer the negative influence of maternal depression with respect to children's social and emotional development. Quality daycare programmes also promote children's intellectual, language and social development.

However, many daycare settings do not meet standards for quality. For example, in one study of early daycare, 56% of settings were observed to be of poor quality, which is hardly surprising, given that childcare staff members are typically untrained and receive poor wages. Governments must be willing to invest in the early education and care of young children, and these investments will result in better school performance in years to come.

Attachment: glossary of terms

attachment: a strong emotional bond that develops over time between an infant and its primary caregiver(s), resulting in a desire to maintain proximity. The attachment bond is thought to form the basis of emotional development and long-term adult relationships.

daycare: an environment in which a child is cared for outside his or her own home by a person (people) other than a relative (e.g. nursery school or childminding).

deprivation: in terms of attachment, deprivation refers to the experience of attachment bond disruption as a result of separation from the attachment figure for a period of time. Note that if there is no bond disruption, then separation not deprivation has occurred.

insecure attachment: a form of attachment which is not optimal for healthy development. Two examples of insecure attachment are avoidant and resistant attachment. Avoidant attachment is shown in the 'strange situation' by indifference when the caregiver leaves, little stranger anxiety and avoidance of contact with the caregiver when he or she returns.

maternal deprivation hypothesis: the suggestion (Bowlby) that separation from a primary caregiver, and thus the breaking of the attachment bond, has long-term negative effects on emotional development.

privation: a lack of any attachment bonds which may lead to permanent emotional damage.

secure attachment: a form of attachment which is optimal for healthy cognitive and emotional development. The securely attached infant is able to function independently because its caregiver provides a secure base. In the 'strange situation', the infant is upset when the caregiver departs but greets him or her positively when the caregiver returns, and is quickly soothed.

You should be able to:
- describe and evaluate the learning theory of attachment
- describe and evaluate Bowlby's explanation of attachment
- describe the characteristics of three types of attachment: secure attachment, insecure-avoidant and insecure-resistant
- describe the procedures used in the 'strange situation'
- explain how the 'strange situation' is used in attachment research
- describe research into cultural variations in attachment
- explain the effects of disruption of attachment and differentiate between disruption of attachment and privation
- describe research into the failure to form attachment (privation)
- describe and evaluate research into the effect of institutional care
- describe and evaluate research into the impact of different forms of daycare on children's social development (aggression)
- describe and evaluate research into the impact of different forms of daycare on children's social development (peer relationships)
- explain how research into attachment and daycare can be applied to influence childcare practices

Knowledge summary

Research methods

Methods and techniques

Specification content

You are expected to demonstrate knowledge and understanding of the following research methods, their advantages and disadvantages:
- *Experimental method, including laboratory, field and natural experiments*
- *Studies using a correlational analysis*
- *Observational techniques*
- *Self-report techniques including questionnaire and interview*
- *Case studies*

Types of research

Psychologists use many methods to conduct research. Each method has advantages and limitations, and the method selected needs to be appropriate for the topic of research. **Quantitative research** uses methods that measure amounts of behaviour, usually by assigning a numeric value to what is being measured (the quantity). **Qualitative research** measures what behaviour is like (the quality) and usually results in descriptive data. Quantitative data are collected as numbers, and qualitative data are collected as descriptions. You need to be able to identify, describe and evaluate the most frequently used research methodologies and designs.

Experimental design

Laboratory experiments

A **laboratory experiment** is a method of conducting research in which researchers try to control all the variables except the one that is changed between the experimental conditions. The variable that is changed is called the **independent variable** (IV) and the effect it may have is called the **dependent variable** (DV). So the IV is manipulated and its effect (the DV) is measured. Laboratory experiments are conducted in controlled and often artificial settings.

> **Examiner tip**
> Students often confuse the IV with the DV — make sure you can define both.

> **Evaluation**

Strengths
- High levels of control in a laboratory experiment allow extraneous variables that might affect the IV or the DV to be minimised. The researcher can be sure that any changes in the DV are the result of changes in the IV.
- High levels of control make it possible to measure the effect of one variable on another. Statements about cause and effect can be made.
- Laboratory experiments can be replicated to check the findings with either the same or a different group of participants.

Weaknesses

- Laboratory experiments may not measure how people behave outside the laboratory in their everyday lives. Some experimental settings and tasks are contrived; hence the findings may have low internal validity.
- Aspects of the experiment may act as cues to behaviour that cause the participants (and the experimenter) to change the way they behave (demand characteristics), sometimes because of what they think is being investigated or how they think they are expected to behave. This can mean that it is not the effect of the IV that is measured, leading to invalid results.

Field experiments

A **field experiment** is a way of conducting research in an everyday environment (e.g. in a school or hospital), where one or more IVs are manipulated by the experimenter and the effect on the DV is measured. One difference between laboratory and field experiments is an increase in the naturalness of the setting and a decrease in the level of control that the experimenter is able to achieve. The key difference is the extent to which participants know they are being studied. Participants are aware of being studied in some field experiments, but this is not true of most, which is why participants' behaviour is more natural.

Evaluation

Strengths

- Field experiments allow psychologists to measure how people behave in their everyday lives. The findings may have high external validity.
- Manipulation of the IV and some level of control make it possible to measure the effect of one variable on another. Statements about cause and effect can be made.
- If participants do not know they are participating in a study, they will be unaware that they are being watched or manipulated. This reduces the probability that their behaviour results from demand characteristics. However, this may not be true of all field experiments; the extent to which demand characteristics are present will vary depending on the experimental setting.

Weaknesses

- It is not always possible to control for extraneous variables that might affect the IV or the DV. The researcher cannot always be sure that any changes in the DV are the result of changes in the IV.
- Field experiments can be difficult to replicate and thus it may not be possible to check the reliability of the findings.
- It may not be possible to ask participants for their informed consent, and participants may be deceived and may not be debriefed, all of which are breaches of British Psychological Society ethical guidelines.

Natural experiments

A **natural experiment** is one in which, rather than being manipulated by the researcher, the IV to be studied is naturally occurring. Some examples of naturally

Examiner tip

You should be able to explain why it might be an advantage to carry out research into eyewitness testimony in the real world rather than in a laboratory.

Knowledge check 16

In an experiment into the primacy recency effect, 25 student participants were seated in a quiet room and given a list of 20 four-letter words printed on a card. All had one minute to memorise the words and then one minute to write down as many as they could remember. Explain whether this is a laboratory experiment or a field experiment.

occurring variables are gender, age, ethnicity, occupation and smoker or non-smoker. When the IV is naturally occurring, participants cannot be randomly allocated between conditions. Just to complicate matters, a natural experiment may take place in a laboratory or in a field experimental setting.

Evaluation

Strengths
- Natural experiments allow psychologists to study the effects of IVs that could be unethical to manipulate.
- When participants are unaware of the experiment, and the task is not contrived, research may have high internal validity.

Weaknesses
- Since participants cannot be allocated randomly between conditions, it is possible that random variables (individual differences other than the IV) can also affect the DV. This may lead to low internal validity.
- Natural experiments can be difficult to replicate with a different group of participants. It may not be possible to check the reliability of the findings.

Correlations and correlational coefficients

Correlation is a statistical technique used to calculate the correlation coefficient in order to quantify the strength of relationship between two variables. An example is whether there is a relationship between aggressive behaviour and playing violent video games. However, studies that use correlational analysis cannot draw conclusions about cause and effect. If a relationship is found between behaving aggressively and playing violent video games, individual differences in personality variables could be one factor that causes both of these. Just because two events (or behaviours) occur together does not mean that one necessarily *causes* the other.

The **correlation coefficient** is a mathematical measure of the degree of relatedness between sets of data. Once calculated, a correlation coefficient will have a value between -1 and $+1$. A **perfect positive correlation**, indicated by $+1$, is where as variable X increases, variable Y increases. A perfect negative correlation, indicated by -1, is where as variable X decreases, variable Y decreases.

Evaluation

Strengths
- Correlational analysis allows researchers to calculate the strength of a relationship between variables as a quantitative measure. A co-efficient of $+0.9$ indicates a strong positive correlation; a coefficient of -0.3 may indicate a weak negative correlation.
- Where a correlation is found, it is possible to make predictions about one variable from the other.

Weaknesses
- Researchers cannot assume that one variable causes the other.
- Correlation between variables may be misleading and can be misinterpreted.

- A lack of correlation may not mean there is no relationship, because the relationship could be non-linear. For example, there is a relationship between physiological arousal and performance, but the relationship is expressed by a curve, not by a straight line. The Yerkes–Dodson curve shows that a little arousal improves performance, but too much reduces performance.

Analysing correlational data

Data can be plotted as points on a scattergram. A line of best fit is then drawn through the points to show the trend of the data.
- If both variables increase together, this is a **positive correlation**.
- If one variable increases as the other decreases, this is a **negative correlation**.
- If no line of best fit can be drawn, there is **no correlation**.

Examiner tip
Sketch three scattergrams, one showing a positive correlation, one showing a negative correlation and one showing no correlation.

Naturalistic observations

When psychologists conduct a **naturalistic observation**, they watch people's behaviour but remain inconspicuous and do nothing to change or interfere with it.

Evaluation

Strengths
- Behaviour can be observed in its usual setting and there are usually no problems with demand characteristics unless the situation in which the participants are being observed has been specially contrived.
- It is useful when researching children or animals.
- It can be a useful way to gather data for a pilot study.

Weaknesses
- No explanation for the observed behaviour is gained because the observer counts instances of behaviour but does not ask participants to explain *why* they acted as they did.
- Observers may 'see what they expect to see' (**observer bias**) or may miss, or misinterpret, behaviour.
- Studies are difficult to replicate.

Knowledge check 18
List two categories of behaviour you might observe if you were carrying out an observation of children's social behaviour.

Interviews and questionnaire surveys

One way to find out about people's behaviour is to ask them, and psychologists often do this. However, one of the main problems with asking questions about behaviour is that we all like others to think well of us. As a result, what we say about our behaviour and how we actually behave may be different. This is called **social desirability bias**.

There are several different ways in which psychologists design and conduct interviews and surveys.

Structured interviews

- All participants are asked the same questions in the same order.
- Structured interviews can be replicated and can be used to compare people's responses.
- They can be time consuming and require skilled researchers. People's responses can be affected by social desirability bias.

Unstructured interviews

- In unstructured interviews, participants can discuss anything freely and the interviewer devises new questions on the basis of answers given previously.
- They provide rich and detailed information, but they are not replicable and people's responses cannot be compared.
- They can be time consuming and people's responses can be affected by social desirability bias. They also require trained interviewers.

Questionnaires

- Questionnaires are usually written, but they can be conducted face to face, or completed over the telephone, or on the internet.
- Printed questionnaires are completed by participants. They are similar to structured interviews in that all participants are asked the same questions in the same order. They usually restrict participants to a narrow range of answers.
- Questionnaires are a practical way to collect a large amount of information quickly and they can be replicated. Problems can arise if the questions are unclear or if they suggest a 'desirable' response, as responses can be affected by social desirability bias. When closed questions are used, participants cannot explain their answers.

Case studies

A case study is a very detailed study into the life and background of one person (or of a small group of people).

Case studies involve looking at past records, such as school and health records, and asking other people about the participant's past and present behaviour. They are often done on people who have unusual abilities or difficulties, e.g. Thigpen and Cleckley's the three faces of Eve.

Evaluation

Strengths
- They give a detailed picture of an individual and help to discover how a person's past may be related to his/her present behaviour.
- They can form a basis for future research.
- By studying the unusual we can learn more about the usual.

Weaknesses
- They can only tell you about one person so findings can never be generalised.
- The interviewer may be biased and/or the interviewee may not tell the truth.
- Retrospective studies may rely on memory, which may be inaccurate or distorted, and past records may be incomplete.

Investigation design

Specification content

You should be familiar with the following features of investigation design:
- *Aims*
- *Hypotheses, including directional and non-directional*
- *Experimental design (independent groups, repeated measures and matched pairs)*
- *Design of naturalistic observations, including the development and use of behavioural categories*
- *Design of questionnaires and interviews (see page 34)*
- *Operationalisation of variables, including independent and dependent variables*
- *Pilot studies*
- *Control of extraneous variables*
- *Reliability and validity*
- *Awareness of the British Psychological Society (BPS) Code of Ethics*
- *Ethical issues and the ways in which psychologists deal with them*
- *Selection of participants and sampling techniques, including random, opportunity and volunteer sampling*
- *Demand characteristics and investigator effects*

This section looks at the ethical guidelines for psychological research and at how psychologists design research, formulate hypotheses, operationalise variables and select participants, and their techniques for assessing and improving validity and reliability.

Ethical research

Psychological research seeks to improve our understanding of human nature, and ethics are standards regarding what is right or wrong. An ethical issue occurs when there is conflict, for example, between what the researcher wants in order to conduct valid or meaningful research and the rights of participants.

Ethical guidelines

The British Psychological Society (BPS) has issued a set of ethical guidelines for research involving human participants. These ethical guidelines are designed to protect the wellbeing and dignity of research participants. The following guidelines are adapted from 'Ethical principles for conducting research with human participants'. The complete text is available on the website of the British Psychological Society (**www.bps.org.uk**).

Introduction
Good psychological research is possible only if there is mutual respect and confidence between investigators and participants. Ethical guidelines are necessary to clarify the conditions under which psychological research is acceptable.

General
In all circumstances, investigators must consider the ethical implications and psychological consequences for the participants in their research. It is essential that the investigation should be considered from the standpoint of all participants; and

foreseeable threats to their psychological wellbeing, health, values or dignity should be eliminated.

Consent

Whenever possible, the investigator should inform all participants of the objectives of the investigation. The investigator should inform the participants of all aspects of the research or intervention that might reasonably be expected to influence willingness to participate. Where research involves any persons under 16 years of age, consent should be obtained from parents or from those *in loco parentis*.

Deception

The misleading of participants is unacceptable if the participants are typically likely to object or show unease once debriefed. Where this is in any doubt, appropriate consultation must precede the investigation. Consultation is best carried out with individuals who share the social and cultural background of the participants. Intentional deception of the participants over the purpose and general nature of the investigation should be avoided whenever possible.

Debriefing

Where the participants are aware that they have taken part in an investigation, when the data have been collected the investigator should provide the participants with any necessary information to complete their understanding of the nature of the research.

Withdrawal from the investigation

At the onset of the investigation, investigators should make plain to participants their right to withdraw from the research at any time, irrespective of whether or not payment or other inducement has been offered. The participant has the right to withdraw retrospectively any consent given, and to require that their own data, including recordings, be destroyed.

Confidentiality

Subject to the requirements of legislation, including the Data Protection Act, information obtained about a participant during an investigation is confidential unless otherwise agreed in advance. Participants in psychological research have a right to expect that information they provide will be treated confidentially and, if published, will not be identifiable as theirs.

Protection of participants

Investigators have a responsibility to protect participants from physical and mental harm during the investigation. Normally, the risk of harm must be no greater than in ordinary life, i.e. participants should not be exposed to risks greater than or additional to those encountered in their normal lifestyles. Where research may involve behaviour or experiences that participants may regard as personal and private, the participants must be protected from stress by all appropriate measures, including the assurance that answers to personal questions need not be given.

Observational research

Studies based upon observation must respect the privacy and psychological wellbeing of the individuals studied. Unless those observed give their consent to being observed, observational research is only acceptable in situations where those observed would expect to be observed by strangers.

Giving advice

If, in the normal course of psychological research, a participant solicits advice concerning educational, personality, behavioural or health issues, caution should be exercised. If the issue is serious and the investigator is not qualified to offer assistance, the appropriate source of professional advice should be recommended.

Examiner tip

Participants are debriefed at the *end* of a research study — not at the beginning.

The dilemma of deception

It can be argued that if participants are not deceived about the true aims of a study, their behaviour is affected and thus does not reflect how they would really behave in their everyday lives (e.g. participants show the effects of demand characteristics).

The dilemma for researchers is to design and conduct research that accurately portrays human behaviour while at the same time ensuring that they do not breach the ethical guidelines. Researchers may solve this dilemma by undertaking a cost–benefit analysis of the research before they commence. However, trying to balance potential benefits against potential costs raises problems:

- It is almost impossible to calculate the costs and benefits before a study, as the researchers cannot predict events accurately.
- Even after a study it is difficult to calculate the costs and benefits, as this may depend on when and who makes the judgement. The value of some research may not become apparent immediately, and participants, and even other researchers, may judge the benefits and costs differently.
- This approach may encourage researchers to ignore the rights of the individual participants on the grounds that 'many more people will benefit'.

The dilemma of informed consent

All participants should be asked to give informed consent prior to taking part in research. However, in some situations where deception may be used, it is not possible to obtain fully informed consent from the participants of the study and psychologists propose the following alternatives.

Presumptive consent

When presumptive consent is gained, people who are members of the population who are to be studied are informed of the details of the study and asked whether, *if they were to participate*, they would consider the research acceptable. Note that these 'potential participants' do not comprise the actual sample of participants.

Prior general consent

This involves asking questions of people who have volunteered to participate, before they are selected to take part. For example:

- Would you mind being involved in a study in which you were deceived?
- Would you mind taking part in a study if you were not informed of its true objectives?
- Would you mind taking part in a study that might cause you some stress?

Participants who say they 'would not mind' may later be selected to participate and it is assumed they have agreed in principle to the conditions of the study.

Examiner tip

Make sure you know the difference between failure to gain informed consent, and deception of participants.

Research methods and ethical issues

Each research method raises different ethical issues, as follows:

- **Laboratory experiment.** Even when told they have the right to withdraw, participants may feel reluctant to do so and may feel they should do things they would not normally do. Participants may be deceived.
- **Field experiment.** It may be difficult to obtain informed consent and participants may not be able to withdraw. It may be difficult to debrief the participants.
- **Natural experiment.** Confidentiality may be a problem, as the sample studied may be identifiable. Where naturally occurring social variables are studied (e.g. family income, ethnicity), ethical issues may arise when drawing conclusions and publishing the findings.
- **Correlational studies.** Ethical issues can arise when researching relationships between socially sensitive variables (e.g. ethnicity and IQ) because published results can be misinterpreted as suggesting 'cause and effect'.
- **Naturalistic observations.** If informed consent is not being gained, people should only be observed in public places and where they would not be distressed to find they were being observed. If the location in which behaviour was observed is identifiable, an ethical issue may arise in terms of protecting confidentiality.
- **Interviews and questionnaires.** Participants should not be asked embarrassing questions (protection from psychological harm) and should be reminded that they do not have to answer any questions if they do not wish to. Protecting confidentiality is important.

Knowledge check 20

A student investigating the relationship between the type of attachment and the quality of young adult relationships designed a questionnaire and circulated it to all the students in her sixth form. From her findings she concluded that participants who had been securely attached as infants had more successful young adult relationships. Identify one ethical issue the researcher would need to consider in this research.

Aims and hypotheses

The **research aim** is a general statement of the purpose of the study and should make clear what the study intends to investigate. The aim states the purpose of the study but is not precise enough to test.

A **hypothesis** states precisely what the researcher believes to be true about the target population. It is often generated from a theory and is a testable statement.

Experimental and alternative hypotheses

The term **experimental hypothesis** is used when experimental research is being conducted (laboratory, field or natural experiments); otherwise the term **alternative hypothesis** is used. The experimental hypothesis states that some difference (or effect) will occur; that the IV will have a significant effect on the DV.

The null hypothesis

The **null hypothesis** is a statement of no difference or of no correlation — the IV does not affect the DV — and is tested by the **inferential statistical test**.

If data analysis forces researchers to reject the null hypothesis, because a significant effect is found, they then accept the experimental hypothesis.

Directional and non-directional hypotheses

The experimental hypothesis can be directional or non-directional.

A **directional hypothesis** is termed a 'one-tailed hypothesis' because it predicts the direction in which the results are expected to go. Directional hypotheses are used when previous research evidence suggests that it is possible to make a clear prediction about the way in which the IV will affect the DV.

A **non-directional hypothesis** is termed a 'two-tailed hypothesis' because, although researchers expect that the IV will affect the DV, they are not sure how.

Experimental design

The independent groups design

Different participants are used in each of the conditions.

Strengths
- No participants are 'lost' between trials.
- Participants can be randomly allocated between the conditions to distribute individual differences evenly.
- There are no practice effects.

Weaknesses
- It needs more participants.
- There may be important differences between the groups to start with that are not removed by the random allocation of participants between conditions.

The repeated measures design

The same group of participants is used in each of the conditions.

Strengths
- It requires fewer participants.
- It controls for individual differences between participants as, in effect, the participants are compared against themselves.

Weaknesses
- It cannot be used in studies in which participation in one condition will affect responses in another (e.g. where participants learn tasks).
- It cannot be used in studies where an order effect would create a problem (see below).

Order effects and counterbalancing

When a repeated measures design is used, problems may arise from participants doing the same task twice. The second time they carry out the task, they may be better than the first time because they have had practice, or worse than the first time because they have lost interest or are tired. If this happens, then an **order effect** is occurring.

Examiner tip

In the exam, when asked to write a hypothesis, students frequently confuse the null hypothesis with the alternative hypothesis. Practise writing alternative and null hypotheses.

Knowledge check 21

Loftus and Palmer carried out two experiments into the effect of leading questions on eyewitness testimony. Write a one-tailed (directional) alternative hypothesis for the second experiment.

One way that researchers control for order effects is to use a **counterbalancing technique**. The group of participants is split and half the group complete condition A followed by condition B; the other half completes condition B followed by condition A. In this way, any order effects are balanced out.

The matched pairs (matched participants) design

Separate groups of participants are used who are matched on a one-to-one basis on characteristics such as age or sex, to control for the possible effect of individual differences.

Evaluation

Strengths
- Matching participants controls for some individual differences.
- It can be used when a repeated measures design is not appropriate (e.g. when performing the task twice would result in a practice effect).

Weaknesses
- A large number of prospective participants is often needed, from which to select matched pairs.
- It is difficult to match on some characteristics (e.g. personality).

Examiner tip

You should be able to explain why a natural experiment cannot use a repeated measures design.

Factors associated with research design

Operationalisation of variables

Operationalisation means being able to define variables in order to manipulate the IV and measure the DV. However, some variables are easier to operationalise than others. For example, performance on a memory test might be operationalised as 'the number of words remembered', but it is more difficult to operationalise how stressed someone may be. You could operationalise stress by measuring physiological arousal, or you could ask participants to rate how stressed they were. Both the IV and the DV need to be precisely operationalised; otherwise, the results may not be valid and cannot be replicated because another researcher would not be able to set up a study to repeat the same measurements.

Knowledge check 22

Loftus and Palmer carried out two experiments into the effect of leading questions on eyewitness testimony. Write an operationalised null hypothesis for the first experiment.

Standardised instructions and procedures

All participants should be told what to do in exactly the same way and all participants should be treated in exactly the same way.

Control of extraneous variables

Any variables that change between the conditions, other than the IV, are difficult to control (e.g. how tired the participants are). Environmental variables that may affect participants' performance, such as the time of day or location, also need to be controlled.

Pilot studies

Research is expensive in terms of both time and money and no piece of research is perfect. To establish whether the design works, that participants can understand the instructions, that nothing has been missed out and that participants are able to do what is asked, a **pilot study** (a trial run with a small number of participants) should be undertaken. This allows researchers to make necessary adjustments and to avoid wasting valuable resources.

Design of naturalistic observations

One of the first things to do when designing a naturalistic observation is to decide how different behaviour should be categorised in order to measure causes and effects. Some categories are relatively easy to identify, e.g. 'walk', 'run', 'sleep', 'smoke', but others are more subtle. The strange situation (Ainsworth and Bell 1970) is an example of how infant behaviour has been categorised so that observers can identify types of attachment. Unless behaviour is clearly categorised, where more than one observer is involved, different observers may interpret the same behaviour in different ways, resulting in low inter-observer reliability.

Preliminary observations

With an observational study, the formulation of the hypothesis and decisions about how best to categorise the behaviour should be undertaken in conjunction with preliminary observations of a small sample of participants.

Sampling behaviour

Once you have decided on your research question and the behavioural categories you will be using, you need to decide who you are going to observe, and how and when.
- **Focal sampling** records the behaviour of one individual at a time. For instance, you might decide to use focal sampling to observe the behaviour of a particular child in a playground, to record all the categories of aggressive incidents during a specified time period. One disadvantage of this method is that your focal 'person' may not engage in any of the behaviour categories of interest. Also, the person you are observing may become aware of your interest.
- **Scan sampling** consists of rapidly scanning a group at specific time intervals to record which behaviour(s) is occurring. This allows observation of a large number of individuals, but has the disadvantage that certain individuals or behaviour may be more conspicuous than others, leading to biased recording.
- **Time sampling** divides the observation period up into sample intervals, e.g. every 2 minutes. A watch can be used to indicate each sample interval. The observer makes a note of the behaviour occurring at each time interval on a pre-prepared tally chart.

Knowledge check 23

You are going to conduct an observation of how students use their mobile phones. List two categories of behaviour you might observe.

Reliability and validity

Reliability

Reliability of results means consistency. In other words, if something is measured more than once, the same effect should result. If my tape measure tells me I am 152 cm tall one day but 182 cm tall the next, the tape measure I am using is not reliable.

Internal reliability refers to how consistently a method measures within itself. For example, my tape measure should measure the same distance between 0 cm and 10 cm as it does between 10 cm and 20 cm. To test for internal reliability, researchers may use the **split-half technique** in which half of the scores are compared with the other half to see how similar they are.

External reliability refers to the consistency of measures over time (i.e. if repeated). For example, personality tests should not give different results if the same person is tested more than once. External reliability can be tested by the **test–retest method**. For example, the same participants can be tested on more than one occasion to see whether their results remain similar.

Inter-observer reliability assesses whether, in an observational study, if several observers are coding behaviour, their codings or ratings agree with each other. To improve reliability, all observers must have clear and operationalised categories of behaviour and must be trained in how to use the system. Inter-observer reliability can be measured using correlational analysis, in which a high positive correlation among ratings indicates that high inter-observer reliability has been established.

Validity

Internal validity refers to the extent to which a measurement technique measures what it is supposed to measure, whether the IV really caused the effect on the DV or whether some other factor was responsible. Experiments may lack internal validity because of demand characteristics or participant reactivity, or because extraneous variables have not been controlled.

Another aspect of internal validity is **mundane realism**, i.e. do the measures used generalise to real life? For example, does a measure of long-term memory based on remembering lists of words generalise to how people really remember past events? Mundane realism is an aspect of internal validity that contributes to external validity.

External validity refers to the validity of a study outside the research situation and provides some idea of the extent to which the findings can be generalised. To assess the external validity of research, three factors should be considered:

- How representative is the sample of participants of the population to which the results are to be generalised (**population validity**)?
- Do the research setting and situation generalise to a realistic real-life setting or situation (**ecological validity**)?
- Do the findings generalise to the past and to the future (**ecological and historical validity**)? For example, it is argued that 50 years ago people were more conformist and obedient.

Examiner tip

Make sure you know the difference between research reliability and research validity.

The participants in research

Selecting participants

When researchers conduct research, the **target population** is the group of people to whom they wish to generalise their findings. The **sample** of participants is the group of people who take part in the study, and a **representative sample** is a sample of people who are representative of the target population. There are several ways in which researchers select a sample.

Random sampling

This involves having the names of the target population and giving everyone an equal chance of being selected. A random sample can be selected by a computer or, in a small population, by selecting names from a hat.

Evaluation

Strength
- A true random sample avoids bias, as every member of the target population has an equal chance of being selected.

Weakness
- It is almost impossible to obtain a truly random sample because not all the names of the target population may be known.

Opportunity sampling

This involves asking whoever is available and willing to participate. An opportunity sample is not likely to be representative of any target population because it will probably comprise friends of the researcher, or students, or people in a specific workplace. The people approached will be those who are local and available. A sample of participants approached 'in the street' is not a random sample of the population of a town. In a random sample, all the people living in a town would have an equal opportunity to participate. In an opportunity sample, only the people present at the time the researcher was seeking participants would be able to participate.

Examiner tip
A sample of people who are approached in a street is not a random sample — do not make this mistake!

Evaluation

Strength
- The researchers can quickly and inexpensively acquire a sample, and face-to-face ethical briefings and debriefings can be undertaken.

Weakness
- Opportunity samples are almost always biased samples, as who participates is dependent on who is asked and who happens to be available at the time.

Volunteer sampling

Volunteer samples mean exactly that: people who volunteer to participate. A volunteer sample may not be representative of the target population because there may be differences between the sort of people who volunteer and those who do not.

Knowledge check 24

Explain why an opportunity sample is almost always a biased sample.

Evaluation

Strength
- The participants should have given their informed consent, will be interested in the research and may be less likely to withdraw.

Weakness
- A volunteer sample may be a biased sample who are not representative of the target population because volunteers may be different in some way from non-volunteers. For example, they may be more helpful (or more curious) than non-volunteers.

Sample representativeness

Researchers wish to apply the findings of their research to learn and explain something about the behaviour of the target population; thus the sample of participants should be a true representation of diversity in the target population. In psychological research, students are often used as participants, but an all-student sample is only representative of a target population of students. Likewise, an all-male sample may only be representative of an all-male target population. If the sample is not representative, the research findings cannot be generalised to the target population.

Researchers also need to decide how many participants are needed, and the number required depends on several factors:
- The sample must be large enough to be representative of the target population.
- If the target population is small, then it may be possible, and sensible, to use the whole population as the sample. However, there is unlikely to be such a small target population in a psychology study.
- The sample needs to be of a manageable size, as too many participants make research expensive and time consuming.
- If the research has important implications (e.g. testing a new drug), the sample size should be larger than it would be in a less important study. In small samples, the individual differences between participants will have a greater effect. If the effect being studied is likely to be small, a larger sample will be required.

The relationship between researchers and participants

Participant effects

When people know they are being studied, their behaviour is affected. Regardless of other variables, as soon as people know their behaviour is of interest, it is likely to change. Some ways in which participation in research can affect behaviour are as follows:
- **The Hawthorne effect.** If people are aware that they are being studied, they are likely to try harder on tasks and pay more attention. This may mean that any findings (e.g. response times) are artificially high, which may lead to invalid conclusions.
- **Demand characteristics.** Sometimes, features of the research situation, the research task and possibly the researcher may give cues to participants as to what

is expected of them or how they are expected to behave, or in some way change participant behaviour. This may lead to response bias, in which participants try to please the experimenter (or deliberately do the opposite), in which case conclusions drawn from the findings may be invalid. Demand characteristics may be reduced if a **single-blind procedure** is used. Here, participants do not know which condition they are participating in, or are given a false account of the experiment. If a single-blind procedure is used, ethical issues arise because fully informed consent cannot be gained. However, if features of the research task cue participants to change their behaviour, a single-blind procedure will not control for this.

- **Social desirability bias.** People usually try to show themselves in the best possible way. So, when answering questions in interviews or questionnaires, they may give answers that are socially acceptable but not truthful. For example, people tend to under-report anti-social behaviour, such as alcohol consumption and smoking, and over-report pro-social behaviour, such as giving to charity.

Investigator and/or experimenter effects

An **investigator** is the person who designs the study and an **experimenter** is the person who conducts the study. They may or may not always be the same person. Researchers may unwittingly affect the results of their research in several ways:

- **Investigator expectancy.** The expectations of the researcher can affect how they design their research and bias how and what they decide to measure, and how the findings are analysed.
- **Experimenter bias.** The experimenter can affect the way participants behave. One way to reduce experimenter effects is to use a **double-blind procedure** in which neither the experimenter nor the participants know what the research hypothesis is.
- **Interviewer effects.** The expectations of the interviewer may lead them to ask only those questions in which they are interested, or to ask leading questions, or they may only focus on answers that match their expectations.
- **Observer bias.** When observing behaviour, observers may make biased interpretations of the meaning of behaviour.

Data analysis and presentation

Specification content

You should be familiar with the following features of data analysis, presentation and interpretation:

- *Presentation and interpretation of quantitative data including graphs, scattergrams and tables*
- *Analysis and interpretation of quantitative data. Measures of central tendency including median, mean, mode. Measures of dispersion including ranges and standard deviation*
- *Analysis and interpretation of correlational data. Positive and negative correlations and the interpretation of correlation coefficients*
- *Presentation of qualitative data*
- *Processes involved in content analysis*

Knowledge check 25

A researcher circulated a questionnaire to parents asking them the following question: *Which of these best describes your child? My child behaves aggressively — Very often; Often, Rarely, Never.* Explain why this question might give rise to social desirability bias.

Quantitative and qualitative data

Experimental research, observations, interviews and questionnaires can result in **quantitative** and/or **qualitative data**.

Strengths of quantitative data
- They are objective.
- Precise measures are used.
- Data are high in reliability.
- It is possible to see patterns in the data.

Weaknesses of quantitative data
- They may lack or lose detail.
- They are often collected in contrived settings.

Strengths of qualitative data
- They are rich and detailed.
- They are collected in real-life settings.
- They can provide information on people's attitudes, opinions and beliefs.

Weaknesses of qualitative data
- They may be subjective.
- They can be an imprecise measure.
- They may be low in reliability.

Examiner tip
You should be able to explain why the strange situation collects qualitative data.

Analysis and interpretation of quantitative data

Measures of **central tendency** and **dispersion** are used to summarise large amounts of data into typical or average values, and to provide information on the variability or spread of the scores.

Measures of central tendency

There are three ways to calculate the average of a set of scores: the mean, the median and the mode.

The mean

To calculate the **mean**, all the scores are added up and the total is divided by the number of the scores.

For example, take the following set of scores: 1, 2, 3, 3, 4, 5, 5, 7, 8, 9.

The mean of this set of scores is 4.7 (47/10).

Evaluation

Strength
- It takes all the values from the raw scores into account.

Weaknesses
- The mean can give a distorted impression if there are unusual (extremely high or low) scores in the data set.
- Often, the mean may have a 'meaningless' decimal point that was not in the original scores (e.g. 2.4 children).

The median

The **median** is the central score in a list of rank-ordered scores. In an odd number of scores, the median is the middle number. In an even-numbered set of scores, the median is the midpoint between the two middle scores.

For example, take the following set of scores: 2, 3, 4, 5, 5, 6, 7, 8, 15, 16.

The median of this set of scores is $(5 + 6)/2 = 5.5$.

The mean of this set of scores is 7.1 (71/10).

Evaluation

Strengths
- The median is not affected by extreme scores.
- It is useful when scores are ordered data (first, second, third etc.)

Weaknesses
- The median does not take account of the values of all of the scores.
- It can be misleading if used in small sets of scores.

The mode

The **mode** is the score that occurs most frequently in a set of scores.

For example, take the following set of scores: 4, 4, 4, 4, 5, 6, 10, 12, 12, 14.

The mode of this set of scores is 4 because it occurs four times (the most frequently).

The median of this set of scores is $(5 + 6)/2 = 5.5$. The mean is 7.5 (75/10). This example shows that each of the measures of central tendency may describe the midpoint of a set of scores differently.

Evaluation

Strengths
- The mode is not affected by extreme scores.
- It is useful when nominal level (frequency level) data are collected.

Weaknesses
- The mode tells us nothing about other scores.
- There may be more than one mode in a set of data.
- NB Nominal level data means that the frequency of instances can only be counted, e.g. 2 red cars, 3 blue cars, 4 silver cars. The data cannot be put into rank order, e.g. because a red car is not more of anything than a blue car.

Examiner tip
Make sure you know the difference between the measures of central tendency: mean, median and mode.

Knowledge check 26
Explain one disadvantage of using the mean as a measure of central tendency of a small sample of scores.

Measures of dispersion

Measures of dispersion tell us about how far spread out they are. The main measures of dispersion are the range and the standard deviation.

Range

To calculate the **range** of a set of scores, subtract the lowest score from the highest score. For example, the range of a set of scores having a lowest score of 10 and a highest score of 24 is 14. The range is a useful measure because if our research has more than one condition, we can compare the range of the scores obtained in each condition. A low range indicates consistency in participant scores and thus low levels of individual differences. A high range indicates variation in participant scores and thus high levels of participant differences. (Note that 'low' or 'high' is relative to the maximum possible range of scores.)

Evaluation

Strengths
- It is easy and quick to work out.
- It includes extreme values.

Weakness
- It may be misleading when there are extremely high or low scores in a set.

Standard deviation

Standard deviation is used to measure how the scores are distributed around the central point (the mean). The greater the standard deviation, the larger the spread of the scores. Standard deviation is useful because when scores are 'normally distributed', about 66% of the scores will lie within 1 standard deviation above or below the mean.

Evaluation

Strengths
- Standard deviation allows for an interpretation of any individual score in a set, and is particularly useful in large sets of scores.
- It is a sensitive measure of dispersion because all the scores are used in its calculation.

Weaknesses
- Standard deviation is not useful when data are not normally distributed.
- It is quite complicated to calculate.

Knowledge check 27

What is the difference between a measure of central tendency and a measure of dispersion?

Graphs and charts

Psychologists use graphs and charts to summarise their data in visual displays. Information provided in graphs and charts makes it easier for others to understand the findings of research.

Bar charts

Bar charts are used when scores are in categories, when there is no fixed order for the items on the x-axis, or can be used to show a comparison of means for continuous data. This bar chart shows the holiday destinations chosen by a sample of 300 families. The bars in bar charts should be the same width but should not touch. The space between the bars illustrates that the variable on the y-axis consists of discrete data.

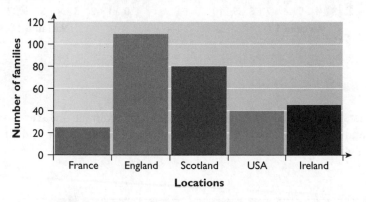

Figure 5 Bar chart showing holiday destinations

Histograms

Histograms show frequencies of scores (how the scores are distributed) using columns. They should be used to display frequency distributions of continuous data and there should be no gaps between the bars. This example shows the exam results (marks) for a class of 30 students in a mock exam marked out of a maximum of 100. The scores have been grouped into ranges of 10 marks.

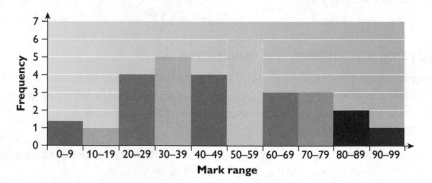

Figure 6 Histogram showing distribution of marks in a mock exam

Scattergrams

Scattergrams are used to depict the result of **correlational analysis**. A scattergram shows at a glance whether there appears to be a positive or negative correlation, or no correlation.

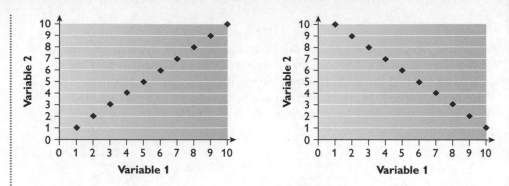

Figure 7 Scattergrams showing positive and negative correlations between two variables

Tables

Psychologists present the findings of research, for example measures of central tendency and dispersions, in tables to make it easy for others to see and interpret the results at a glance.

Example

Correct answers in a maths test	Condition A male	Condition B female
Mean	12.11	15.23
Median	11	14
Range	6	4
Standard deviation	2.25	3.5

Content analysis

This involves the coding and analysis of qualitative data.

Analysing and presenting qualitative data

In interviews and observations, qualitative data might result from video or audio recordings or written notes. Likewise, qualitative data can result when open questions are asked in interviews or questionnaires, or when participants are invited to explain why they behave in a certain way.

It is important when analysing qualitative data that researchers avoid subjective or biased misinterpretations. Misinterpretation can be avoided by:

- using accurate language to operationalise the variables to be measured — for example, if observing play-fighting in children, an operationalised definition might be 'hitting while smiling' (though counting the frequency of this would be quantitative data)
- using a team of observers who have verified that they have achieved inter-observer reliability
- converting qualitative data into quantitative data; one way to do this is by coding the data

Coding qualitative data

A sample of qualitative data is collected – for example, from the interviewee, from magazines or newspapers, or from the notes or recordings of an observation.

Coding units are identified in order to categorise the data. A coding unit could be specific words or phrases that are looked for (the operationalised definitions).

The coding units may then be counted to see how frequently they occur. The resulting frequency of occurrence is a form of quantitative data.

Research methods: glossary of terms

correlations: a statistical technique used to calculate the correlation coefficient in order to quantify the strength of relationship between two variables.

counterbalancing: a way of controlling for order effects by having half the participants complete condition A followed by condition B; the other participants complete condition B followed by condition A.

demand characteristics: aspects of the experiment may act as cues to behaviour that cause the participants (and the experimenter) to change the way they behave.

dependent variable (DV): the effect of the IV, or what is measured, in an experiment.

ethical guidelines: the British Psychological Society (BPS) has issued a set of ethical guidelines for research involving human participants. These ethical guidelines are designed to protect the wellbeing and dignity of research participants.

external validity: the validity of a study outside the research situation and the extent to which the findings can be generalised.

field experiment: a way of conducting research in an everyday environment, e.g. in a school or hospital, where one or more IVs are manipulated by the experimenter and the effect it may have (the DV) is measured.

Hawthorne effect: when people are aware that they are being studied, they are likely to try harder on tasks and pay more attention.

hypothesis: this states precisely what the researcher believes to be true about the target population and is a testable statement.

independent groups design: different participants are used in each of the conditions.

independent variable (IV): the variable that is manipulated (changed) between experimental conditions.

internal validity: the extent to which a measurement technique measures what it is supposed to measure, whether the IV really caused the effect on the DV or whether some other factor was responsible.

inter-observer reliability: whether, in an observational study, if several observers are coding behaviour, their codings or ratings agree with each other.

Knowledge check 28

In a study of anti-social behaviour, a psychologist asked primary school teachers to describe children's behaviour they observed in the playground and then used content analysis to analyse the descriptions. Suggest two behavioural categories that could be used in this content analysis.

laboratory experiment: a method of conducting research in which researchers try to control all the variables except the one that is changed between the experimental conditions.

matched participants design: separate groups of participants are used who are matched on a one-to-one basis on characteristics such as age or sex, to control for the possible effect of individual differences.

natural experiment: an experimental method, in which, rather than being manipulated by the researcher, the IV to be studied is naturally occurring. Some examples of naturally occurring variables are gender and age.

naturalistic observations: a research method in which psychologists watch people's behaviour but remain inconspicuous and do nothing to change or interfere with it.

null hypothesis: a statement of no difference or of no correlation — the IV does not affect the DV. It is tested by the inferential statistical test.

operationalisation of variables: being able to define variables in order to manipulate the IV and measure the DV, e.g. performance on a memory test might be operationalised as 'the number of words remembered from a list of words'.

opportunity sampling: asking whoever is available and willing to participate. An opportunity sample is not likely to be representative of any target population because it will probably comprise friends of the researcher, or students, or people in a specific workplace.

order effects: when a repeated measures design is used, problems may arise from participants doing the same task twice because the second time they carry out the task, they may be better than the first time because they have had practice or worse than the first time because they have lost interest or are tired.

pilot studies: a trial run of research with a small number of participants to researchers to make necessary adjustments and to save wasting valuable resources.

qualitative data: rich and detailed data collected in real-life settings, for example people's subjective opinions.

quantitative data: objective, precise, usually numerical, data that can be statistically analysed.

random sampling: having the names of the target population and giving everyone an equal chance of being selected.

reliability: reliability of results means consistency. In other words, if something is measured more than once, the same effect should result.

repeated measures design: the same group of participants is used in each of the conditions.

research aim: a general statement of the purpose of the study. It should make clear what the study intends to investigate.

self-report methods: a way of finding out about people's behaviour by interviewing them or by asking them to fill out questionnaires.

structured interviews: participants are asked the same questions in the same order.

social desirability bias: when people try to show themselves in the best possible way, so that when answering questions in interviews or questionnaires they give answers that are socially acceptable but are not truthful.

unstructured interviews: participants can discuss anything freely and the interviewer devises new questions on the basis of answers previously given.

volunteer sampling: participants volunteer to participate, e.g. by responding to advertisements.

You should be able to:

- describe and evaluate experimental research methods, including laboratory, field and natural experiments
- describe and evaluate non-experimental research methods, including correlational analysis, observational techniques, self-report techniques including questionnaire and interview, and case studies

You should be confident you can identify and describe features of investigation design:

- aims
- hypotheses, including directional and non-directional
- experimental design (independent groups, repeated measures and matched pairs)
- design of naturalistic observations, including the development and use of behavioural categories
- design of questionnaires and interviews
- operationalisation of variables, including independent and dependent variables
- pilot studies and control of extraneous variables

You should be able to:

- define reliability and validity and differentiate between these
- describe the British Psychological Society (BPS) Code of Ethics and recognise ethical issues and the ways in which psychologists deal with them
- describe and evaluate sampling techniques, including random, opportunity and volunteer sampling
- define demand characteristics and explain ways by which an investigator may affect research
- define quantitative and qualitative data and differentiate between these
- present quantitative data in visual diagrams including graphs, scattergrams and tables
- calculate measures of central tendency including median, mean, mode and know when to use these
- calculate measures of dispersion including ranges and standard deviation and be able to explain why dispersions are useful
- analyse and interpretet correlational data and differentiate between positive and negative correlations
- know what is meant by a correlation coefficient and how to interpret these
- describe ways of analysing qualitative data and the processes involved in content analysis

Knowledge summary

Questions & Answers

This section contains nine questions: four on cognitive psychology, four on developmental psychology and one structured question (6 parts) on research methods.

The section is structured as follows:
- sample questions in the style of the unit exam
- example student responses at grade B, C and D levels (student A), demonstrating strengths and weaknesses and the potential for improvement
- example student responses at grade A level (student B), demonstrating thorough knowledge, good understanding and an ability to deal with the data presented in the question

Examiner comments

All student responses are followed by examiner comments, which are preceded by the icon ℮. Examiner comments may indicate where credit is due, strengths in the answer, areas for improvement, specific problems, common errors, lack of clarity, irrelevance, mistakes in the meaning of terms and/or misinterpretation of the question. Comments indicate how the answers might be marked in an exam, using the mark allocations listed on pages 56–57.

The examination

Assessment objectives: AO1, AO2 and AO3 skills

The requirements of the three assessment objectives that you will be examined on are outlined in the table below.

AO1	Recognise, recall and show understanding of scientific knowledge; select, organise and communicate relevant information in a variety of forms.
AO2	Analyse and evaluate scientific knowledge; apply knowledge and processes to unfamiliar situations; assess the validity, reliability and credibility of scientific information.
AO3	Describe ethical, safe and skilful practical techniques and processes; know how to make, record and communicate valid observations; analyse, interpret, explain and evaluate the methodology and investigative activities in a variety of forms.

Questions

Unit 1 is assessed in an examination lasting 1 hour 30 minutes and you must answer all the questions. Section A comprises questions on cognitive psychology and research methods. Section B comprises questions on developmental psychology and research methods.

The following are examples of the types of question that may be used to assess your AO1, AO2 and AO3 skills.

AO1 questions

Outline key features of the working memory model.   *(6 marks)*

Describe the multi-store model of memory.   *(6 marks)*

Outline the behavioural explanation of attachment formation.   *(6 marks)*

AO2 questions

Explain one strength of the working memory model.   *(4 marks)*

Explain how the behavioural explanation of attachment differs from Bowlby's theory of attachment.   *(4 marks)*

AO1 + AO2 question

Outline and evaluate research into the effects of daycare on social development (e.g. aggression, peer relations).   *(AO1, 6 marks + AO2, 6 marks)*

AO3 questions

Explain why studies of eyewitness testimony have been criticised as lacking validity. *(5 marks)*

Explain one ethical issue relevant to the observational studies of young children. *(2 marks)*

Effective examination performance

Read the question carefully because marks are awarded only for the specific requirements of the question *as it is set*. Don't waste valuable time answering a question that you *wish* had been set.

Make a brief plan before you start writing an extended answer. This plan can be a simple list of points, but you must know what, and how much, you plan to write. Time management in exams is vital.

Sometimes a question asks you to outline something. You should practise doing this in order to develop the skill of précis.

Be aware of the difference between AO1, AO2 and AO3 questions. You can lose marks if you treat AO2 questions as an opportunity to write more descriptive (AO1) content. Read the question injunction carefully and note the relevant skill requirement in your question plan (e.g. outline = AO1, describe = AO1, evaluate = AO2).

In AO1 questions, marks are awarded in bands for the amount of relevant material presented (e.g. low marks for brief or inappropriate material; high marks for accurate and detailed material).

In AO2 questions and/or the AO2 component of AO1 + AO2 questions, marks are awarded in bands for the amount, level and effectiveness of critical commentary (e.g.

low marks for superficial consideration of a restricted range of issues; high marks for a good range of ideas and specialist terms, and effective use of material addressing a broad range of issues).

AO3 questions require you to demonstrate a thorough understanding of methods by which psychologists conduct research. You must be able to describe ethical, safe and skilful practical techniques and processes; know how to make, record and communicate valid observations; and how to analyse, interpret, explain and evaluate the methodology and investigative activities.

How the marks are awarded

AO1 Knowledge and understanding	AO2 and AO3 Application of knowledge and understanding
6 marks: accurate and reasonably detailed Accurate and reasonably detailed description that demonstrates sound knowledge and understanding of relevant research. There is appropriate selection of material to address the question.	**6 marks: effective evaluation** Effective use of material to address the question and provide informed commentary. Effective evaluation of research. Broad range of issues and/or evidence in reasonable depth, or a narrower range in greater depth. Clear expression of ideas, good range of specialist terms, few errors of grammar, punctuation or spelling.
5–4 marks: less detailed but generally accurate Less detailed but generally accurate description that demonstrates relevant knowledge and understanding of research. There is some evidence of selection of material to address the question.	**5–4 marks: reasonable evaluation** Material is not always used effectively but a reasonable commentary is produced. Reasonable evaluation of research. A range of issues and/or evidence in limited depth, or a narrower range in greater depth. Reasonable expression of ideas, a range of specialist terms, some errors of grammar, punctuation and spelling.
3–2 marks: basic Basic description that demonstrates some relevant understanding but lacks detail and may be muddled. There is little evidence of selection of material to address the question.	**3–2 marks: basic evaluation** The use of material provides only a basic commentary. Basic evaluation or research. Superficial consideration of a restricted range of issues and/or evidence. Expression of ideas lacks clarity, some specialist terms used, errors of grammar, punctuation and spelling detract from clarity.
1 mark: very flawed or inappropriate Very brief or flawed description demonstrating very little knowledge. Selection and presentation of information is largely or wholly inappropriate.	**1 mark: rudimentary evaluation** The use of material provides only a rudimentary commentary. Evaluation of research is just discernible or absent. Expression of ideas poor, few specialist terms used, errors of grammar, punctuation and spelling often obscure the meaning.
0 marks: no creditworthy material	**0 marks: no creditworthy material**

Mark allocations for an AO1, 6-mark question

Example

Outline key features of the working memory model.   *(6 marks)*

Marks	Criteria for AO1
	Recognise, recall and show understanding of scientific knowledge, select, organise and communicate relevant information.
6	Accurate and reasonably detailed outline of *(working memory model)* that demonstrates sound knowledge and understanding of *(working memory model)* and appropriate selection of material.
5–4	Less detailed but generally accurate outline of *(working memory model)* that demonstrates knowledge and understanding and some evidence of selection of material.
3–2	Basic outline of *(working memory model)* and limited evidence of selection of material.
1	Brief or flawed outline of *(working memory model)* demonstrating very little knowledge.
0	No creditworthy material.

Mark allocations for an AO2, 6-mark question

Example

Outline and evaluate research into the effects of daycare on social development (e.g. aggression, peer relations). *(AO1, 6 marks + AO2, 6 marks)*

Marks	Criteria for AO2
	Analyse and evaluate scientific knowledge, apply knowledge and processes to unfamiliar situations, assess the validity, reliability and credibility of scientific information.
6	**Effective evaluation:** effective use of material, broad range of issues and/or evidence in reasonable depth, or narrower range of issues in greater depth, good range of specialist terms, clear expression of ideas, few errors of grammar, spelling or punctuation.
5–4	**Reasonable evaluation:** material used less effectively but a range of issues/evidence in limited depth or fewer issues in greater depth, a range of specialist terms, some errors of grammar, punctuation or spelling.
3–2	**Basic evaluation:** superficial consideration of a limited range of issues and/or evidence, lack of clarity in use of specialist terms, or spelling, punctuation or grammar errors detract from clarity.
1	**Rudimentary evaluation:** evaluation of material is just discernible, expression of ideas is poor, few specialist terms.
0	**No creditworthy material.**

Question 1 Cognitive psychology (1)

Outline key features of the working memory model. (6 marks)

ⓔ Question injunction = outline. This question requires you to show AO1 skills. You need to demonstrate your understanding of the key features of the working memory model. You are not required to give evidence that supports the model or the strengths and limitations of the model. You are not expected to provide more than 5–6 minutes of writing. To outline the model, you should identify the components of the model and provide a brief outline of their function.

Answers

Student A

The working memory model is a model of STM having three parts. The central executive. ⓐ The phonological loop processes speech-based information. The visuospatial working area processes visual information.

ⓔ **3/6 marks awarded.** This answer provides accurate information. Student A provides a basic outline of the working memory model, shows some understanding that the working memory model is a model of STM and gives an accurate but basic outline of the three component parts. The weakness of this answer is that it is like a list and ⓐ gives no information about the function of the central executive.

Student B

The working memory model proposes that STM is an active processor in which the central executive 'attends to and works on' either speech-based information or visually coded information. ⓐ The central executive processes information from all sensory routes; this process is 'attention-like', having limited capacity. ⓑ The articulatory–phonological loop processes speech-based information. The phonological store focuses on incoming speech perception and the articulatory process focuses on speech production. ⓒ The visuospatial working area is where spatial and visual information is processed. ⓓ

ⓔ **5–6/6 marks awarded.** In (a) to (d) the student provides an accurate and more detailed outline of the working memory model that demonstrates a sound understanding of all three components of the model and of their function.

Question 2 Cognitive psychology (2)

Describe the multi-store model of memory. (6 marks)

ⓔ Question injunction = describe. This question requires you to show AO1 skills. You need to demonstrate your understanding of the multi-store model of memory by writing a detailed and accurate description. You are not required to give evidence that supports the model or the strengths and limitations of the model. You are not expected to provide more than 5–6 minutes of writing. To describe the model, you should identify the components of the model and provide a brief outline of their function.

Answers

Student A

The multi-store model proposes that memory consists of different stores, sensory memory, short-term memory (STM) and long-term memory (LTM). Information is passed from STM to LTM by rehearsing information. a Like when we repeat a telephone number so we don't forget it.

ⓔ **2–3/6 marks awarded.** Student A provides a basic description of the multi-store model and gives an accurate but very basic outline of the three memory stores. a Credit would be given for the accurate suggestion that information is passed from STM to LTM by rehearsal. The weakness of the answer is that it gives no information about the functions of the three memory stores or the differences between them.

Student B

The multi-store model suggests that memory consists of different stores, sensory memory, short-term memory (STM) and long-term memory (LTM). a Sensory memory is where information enters the system through our senses (e.g. our eyes and ears). If the information in sensory memory is attended to, it will be passed to the STM store which has limited capacity for about seven chunks of information. b Verbal rehearsal maintains information in STM, but STM has limited duration, thus the information may be lost if it is displaced by new incoming information. c Information is passed from STM to LTM by rehearsing the information and LTM has unlimited capacity and duration so the information may be remembered for a lifetime. d

ⓔ **5–6/6 marks awarded.** Student B provides a thorough, accurate and detailed description of the multi-store model of memory, which in a to d demonstrates a sound understanding of all three components of the model, of their function, of the characteristics of STM and LTM, and of the differences between STM and LTM.

Question 3 **Cognitive psychology (3)**

Explain one strength of the working memory model. (4 marks)

ⓔ Question injunction = explain. This question requires you to show AO2 skills. You need to demonstrate your understanding by writing a detailed and accurate explanation of one strength of the model. The question does not require you to describe the model. One mark will be awarded for accurate identification of a strength and further marks will be awarded for elaboration.

Possible strengths include:

- It receives support from empirical evidence.
- It shows that STM is more complex than is suggested by the multi-store model.
- It shows that STM is better seen as a number of independent processing systems rather than as a single store.
- It explains how we have the ability to perform two tasks at the same time if the two tasks use different processes.

You are not expected to provide more than about 4 minutes of writing. In your answer, you should first identify the strength and then explain it — perhaps by making a comparison to the multi-store model, or by giving an example.

Answers

Student A

One strength of the working memory model is that it suggests rehearsal as an optional process. This is more realistic than the multi-store model, especially since we do not rehearse everything that we remember. a

e **2/4 marks awarded.** Student A provides a basic and accurate explanation of one strength of the working memory model. A mark would be awarded for the identification of the strength; a further mark would be awarded for a the basic explanation that we do not rehearse everything that we remember. The weakness of this answer is that it is a very brief explanation.

Student B

One strength of the working memory model is that it can explain how we can successfully do two tasks at the same time if the tasks involve different stores, a but why we have trouble performing two tasks at the same time if the tasks involve the same stores. b For instance, because the articulatory–phonological loop and the visuospatial scratchpad both have limited capacity to process information, when participants are asked to perform two tasks, using the same system at the same time (e.g. speaking and reading), their performance will be affected because both these tasks use the articulatory–phonological loop. c

e **4/4 marks awarded.** Student B provides an accurate and detailed explanation of one strength of the working memory model, demonstrating a sound understanding. A mark would be awarded for a the accurate identification of the strength, and a further 1 or 2 marks for b the elaboration. An additional 1 or 2 marks would be awarded for the detailed example given, c which shows a clear understanding of the different functions of the components proposed by the working memory model.

Question 4 Cognitive psychology (4)

Explain why studies of eyewitness testimony have been criticised as lacking validity. (5 marks)

ⓔ Question injunction = explain. This question relates to research methods and requires you to show AO3 skills. Possible answers could focus on external validity (ecological validity):

- the laboratory environment in which much research into EWT is undertaken
- participants not being as emotionally aroused as they would be in a real incident and not feeling the same sense of responsibility
- the lack of realism in tasks when participants watch video films as compared to observing a real event

You are not expected to provide more than about 5 minutes of writing. You need to write an explanation that demonstrates your understanding of validity and your knowledge of the studies.

Answers

Student A

Loftus and Palmer conducted a laboratory experiment into the effect of leading questions on eyewitness testimony. Participants were asked to watch a video and then some participants were asked how fast the cars were travelling when they *bumped* into each other but other participants were asked how fast the cars were going when they *smashed* into each other. Participants who were asked the question with the word *smashed* reported the cars travelling faster. ⓐ This research has low ecological validity because the participants watched a film which is not like watching a real accident. ⓑ

ⓔ **1/5 marks awarded.** Student A has made the common error of spending too much time in ⓐ describing the Loftus and Palmer research (AO1 skills), which is not required by the question. ⓑ Only the final sentence addresses the question, and this is a very brief statement rather than an explanation. The student does not explain why watching a film is not like watching a real accident. Hence the student has wasted time on unnecessary description and has not focused on the question.

Student B

Ecological validity (external validity) refers to the extent to which the procedures used in research are realistic in that they could happen in real life, and the extent to which the sample of participants is representative of the type of people who might be eyewitnesses to a real incident. ⓐ Much of the research into EWT has been laboratory experiments (e.g. the Loftus and Palmer research into the effect of leading questions on EWT). ⓑ This research can be criticised as having low ecological validity, because when watching a video film, participants will not be as emotionally aroused as they would be in a real incident (no surprise or danger) and they will not feel the same sense of responsibility when they answer questions about what they have witnessed. ⓒ Also, many laboratory experiments use samples of all students, which reduces the ecological validity because students spend much of their time memorising information, which would not be the case with witnesses to a real incident. ⓓ

e **5/5 marks awarded.** Student B provides an accurate and detailed explanation of why some research lacks ecological validity. The student starts by demonstrating a good understanding in ⬛ of the term 'ecological validity'. Then the student gives an appropriate example of research and in ⬛, ⬛ and ⬛ writes an accurate, clear and detailed explanation of why this research may be criticised as lacking ecological validity. The strength of this answer is that the student has not wasted time on unnecessary description and has focused on the question.

Question 5 Developmental psychology (1)

Describe the behavioural explanation of attachment formation. (6 marks)

e Question injunction = describe. This question requires you to show AO1 skills. You need to demonstrate your understanding of the main features of the behavioural explanation of attachment and your description should demonstrate that you understand the behavioural perspective. You are not required to give evidence that supports the behavioural explanation or the strengths and limitations of the explanation. You do not need to provide more than 5–6 minutes of writing. Answers could focus on the following:

- Attachment is learned through conditioning.
- Attachment bonds are developed because of the association between the pleasure of receiving food and the person who is feeding the infant.
- Attachment bonds are developed because of operant conditioning — positive reinforcement because being close to the caregiver gives pleasure.

Answers

Student A

The behavioural theory proposes that the infant's attachment bond, with his or her caregiver, can be explained in terms of operant conditioning — the reinforcement (pleasure) arising from the satisfaction of basic needs such as food and drink. The mother (or caregiver) provides pleasure and the infant learns to associate pleasure with the caregiver. ⬛

e **3–4/6 marks awarded.** Student A provides a basic description of the behavioural explanation of the development of attachment. Credit would be given for ⬛ the fairly brief, but accurate, description of how operant conditioning may explain the development of the attachment bond. The weakness of this answer is that, although accurate, it is very brief.

Student B

The behavioural explanation proposes that a child's attachment bond develops through learning and that the infant's attachment bond with his or her caregiver can be explained in terms of operant conditioning. ⬛ Based on operant conditioning, infants feel discomfort when they are hungry and so desire food to remove the discomfort. ⬛ They learn that if they cry, their caregiver feeds them and the discomfort is removed. ⬛ This is negative reinforcement: the consequences of behaviour (crying) lead to something unpleasant ceasing (feeling hungry stops). ⬛

Thus, the behaviour of 'being close' to the caregiver is reinforced, which in turn leads to the attachment behaviour of distress on being separated from the caregiver. ■

ⓔ 5–6/6 marks awarded. Student B provides an accurate and detailed description of the behavioural explanation of the development of attachments. In ■ to ■ the answer demonstrates a sound understanding of the key features of learning theory and how this can be applied to explain the development of the key features of attachment. The strength of this answer is in ■ and ■ in the accurate use of psychological terminology.

Question 6 **Developmental psychology (2)**

Explain how Bowlby's explanation of attachment differs from the behavioural explanation of attachment.
(5 marks)

ⓔ Question injunction = explain. This question requires you to show AO2 skills. You need to demonstrate your understanding by writing a detailed and accurate explanation of the difference between Bowlby's theory and behavioural explanations of attachment. The question does not require you to describe the explanations. To gain full marks you need to explain the consequences or implications of the difference you suggest. One mark will be awarded for accurate identification of a difference and further marks will be awarded for elaboration.

Possible differences include the following:
- According to Bowlby, infants are innately programmed to form attachment, so attachment is biological rather than learned.
- The behavioural explanation suggests no critical period — attachments can be learned and relearned.
- The behavioural explanation does not suggest that attachment is the basis, or template, for future relationships and thus does not predict negative long-term consequences following disruption of attachment.

You are not expected to provide more than about 5 minutes of writing. In your answer you should first identify one or more differences and then explain the implications of the difference(s).

Answers

Student A

Bowlby suggests that infants are biologically programmed to form attachments and thus that attachments are innate (nature) rather than nurture. ■

ⓔ 1–2/5 marks awarded. Student A outlines a feature of the evolutionary explanation — but while the answer is accurate, it is little more than a statement. ■ Only the final part of the sentence touches on a difference between the two explanations. The weakness of this answer is that the student has not elaborated and explained the implications of the difference that he or she has identified.

Student B

The main difference between Bowlby's and the behaviourist explanation is that Bowlby suggests that infants are biologically programmed to develop attachments and thus that attachments form because of innate biological characteristics while the behavioural explanation suggests that attachments develop because of nurture (learning from experience). a Bowlby also suggests that there may be a critical period in which attachment bonds may develop but behavioural theorists suggest that attachment bonds should be able to be learned (and relearned) at any age. b

e **5/5 marks awarded.** Student B provides an accurate and detailed explanation, demonstrating an understanding of the difference between the theories, and of the implications of these differences. Although in a and b the student focuses on one difference, the strength of this answer is that the student uses psychological terminology accurately to demonstrate that he or she has a good understanding of the key features of both Bowlby's and the behavioural explanation.

Question 7 Developmental psychology (3)

(a) Explain one ethical problem associated with an observational study of children. (3 marks)

(b) Explain one practical problem associated with an observational study of children. (3 marks)

e Question injunction = explain. Because this question relates to research methods, this assesses your AO3 skills. For question (a) you need to demonstrate your understanding of the issues involved in conducting ethical research. For question (b) you need to demonstrate your understanding of the practical problems that can arise while conducting research. For each question, 1 mark would be awarded for the identification of a relevant problem and up to a further 2 marks for the explanation.

Ethical problems might include:
- informed consent
- failure to protect, in that the absence of the mother causes distress
- confidentiality
- the right to withdraw might bias the sample

Practical problems might include:
- reliable categorisation of behaviours
- correct interpretation of behaviours
- noticing and recording behaviour without bias; behaviour sampling

Answers

Student A

(a) One ethical problem when observing children is that a parent must be asked to give informed consent and they might not want to.

(b) One practical problem is that children move around a lot, so the observer might not see all the behaviour.

e **1/3 marks awarded** for each answer. Student A identifies an appropriate problem in both answers, but the weakness of these answers is that the student has not elaborated and explained the implications of the problems that he or she has identified.

Student B

(a) One ethical problem when observing children is that having given their informed consent the parent must be allowed the right to withdraw the child from the research, **a** and if they choose to withdraw their child, this may result in a biased sample of participants. **b**

(b) One practical problem is that children move around a lot, **a** so more than one observer will be needed to ensure that the results are reliable. **b** Having more than one observer means that the behaviour to be observed must be clearly categorised in terms of what is to be 'counted' to ensure that both observers are counting the same behaviours (inter-observer reliability). **c**

e **3/3 marks awarded** for each answer. Student B identifies an appropriate problem in both answers. In part (a) the student identifies the problem in **a** and in **b** explains the effect of this problem. In part (b) the student identifies a problem in **a** and then in **b** and **c** gives an extended explanation demonstrating an understanding of the implications of the problems identified. The strength of this answer is that the student uses psychological terminology accurately to demonstrate that he or she has a good understanding of ethical and practical problems that can arise when involving young children in observational research.

Question 8 **Developmental psychology (4)**

Describe and evaluate research into the effects of daycare on social development (e.g. aggression, peer relations).   (6 marks + 6 marks)

e Question injunction = describe and evaluate. This question assesses both AO1 and AO2 skills, with 6 marks available for each.

For the 'describe' (AO1) part of the question, you should briefly describe research into the effects of daycare. You do not need to provide more than 5–6 minutes of writing. There are a wide range of studies that could be included, such as the following:

- Kagan et al. (1980) studied the effects of nursery care and found no significant differences between the groups studied. They concluded that daycare was not harmful.
- Belsky and Rovine (1988) found that children who had been in daycare had insecure attachment types but that those who had not experienced daycare were more likely to be securely attached. It was concluded that daycare has a negative effect on social development.
- Shea (1981) studied two groups of 3–4-year-old children. One group attended nursery school for 5 days each week and the other group attended just twice each week. The children were assessed for their social skills. Both groups increased their social skills, were less aggressive and interacted more with others. It was concluded that daycare has a positive effect on social development.

For the 'evaluate' (AO2) part of the question, you might focus on the strengths and weaknesses of the methods used in the research you have outlined, and/or evaluate the findings and implications. For high marks you need to express your ideas clearly, using appropriate psychological terminology, to demonstrate clear understanding. You can address either a broad range of issues in reasonable depth or a narrower range of issues in greater depth. Make sure that you focus on the question of the effects of daycare on social development.

For this split AO1 /AO2 question, you should write a quick plan before you write your answer. You need to provide about 6 minutes of content for the AO1 section and 6 minutes of content for the AO2 section. Don't waste time writing 'all you know about research into daycare' — your answer should provide as much AO2 content as AO1 content.

Answers

Student A

AO1 section
Shea (1981) studied two groups of children who attended nursery school. One group attended for 5 days each week and the other group attended twice a week and the researchers measured their social skills. Both groups were less aggressive and interacted more with others but the social skills of the 5-days-a-week group improved more rapidly. It was concluded that daycare has a positive effect on social development. Mayall and Petrie (1983) studied childminders in London. The study found that the quality of care varied; some childminders were excellent but others didn't provide a stimulating environment so the children in their care failed to thrive.

ⓔ **2–3/6 marks awarded.** Student A gives a basic description that demonstrates some relevant knowledge and understanding but which lacks detail. There is some evidence of selection of material to address the question, but the selection of the Mayall and Petrie (1983) study of childminding is a weakness because this study does not focus on social development. To improve the answer, the student could have presented a more appropriate second study.

AO2 section
The Shea study has high ecological validity because the children were in a nursery school. ⓐ However, other factors might have affected the children's behaviour so the study may have low validity. Also there was only a small sample of children involved so the results cannot be generalised to all children. ⓑ The research into childminders also cannot be generalised to all childminders because there was only a small sample of childminders involved.

ⓔ **2–3/6 marks awarded.** In ⓐ and ⓑ Student A provides only a basic commentary and superficial consideration of a restricted range of issues. Some specialist terms are used, but the issues are not elaborated or fully explained. The student attempts to evaluate the quoted research but fails to evaluate the effects of daycare on social development.

Student B

AO1 section

Bowlby theorised that daycare would cause permanent damage to the emotional health of children, but more recently it has been suggested that daycare has benefits for poor children so they can start school having equal opportunities with their peers. As a result there has been much research into whether and how the experience of daycare affects the social development of children. **a**

Kagan et al. (1980) set up their own nursery school in Boston (USA) to study the effects of nursery care. The study (a natural experiment) looked at 33 infants who had attended the nursery full time from the age of $3\frac{1}{2}$ months and compared them with a matched control group of children who stayed at home. **b** The children were assessed for more than 2 years on attachment and sociability. No significant differences were found between the groups and it was concluded that daycare was not harmful. However, in another natural experiment, **c** Belsky and Rovine (1988) also studied the effect of daycare on social development in two groups of children. One group had experienced no daycare and the other had experienced at least 20 hours of daycare each week before their first birthday. The children were placed in the strange situation to test how strong their attachments were. **d** The children who had been in daycare were said to have insecure attachment types, but those who had not experienced daycare were more likely to be securely attached. It was concluded that daycare has a negative effect on social development.

In another study, **e** Shea (1981) studied two groups of children aged between 3 and 4. One group attended nursery school for 5 days each week and the other group attended just twice each week. During 10 weeks of nursery the children were assessed for their social skills. **f** Both groups increased their social skills, were less aggressive and interacted more with others, but the social skills of the 5-days-a-week group improved more rapidly. It was concluded that daycare has a positive effect on social development. **g**

e **6/6 marks awarded.** Student B in the AO1 section makes an admirable selection of material describing the effect of daycare on social development. The student provides an accurate and detailed description of appropriate research, demonstrating his or her sound knowledge and understanding. In **b** to **g** there is appropriate selection of material to address the question and the presentation is clear and coherent. Although **a** the first paragraph is an effective start to the answer, the student could have shortened this to save time because most students will struggle to write 300 words in 5–6 minutes.

AO2 section

One of the strengths of the research studies quoted is that they have high external validity. All of the children studied did experience daycare as part of their everyday lives. Also, in the quoted studies the researchers provided a matched control group of children who experienced either no daycare or a different pattern of daycare — thus facilitating comparisons of social development. **a** However, although the children were matched for age, many factors may influence how daycare affects a child, including the child's temperament and his/her home background. **b** It is thus difficult to isolate daycare as the single factor affecting a child's social development because of the wide range of individual differences involved. In fact, █ Kagan et al. (1980) suggest that when considering the effects of daycare, a double standard is applied, where daycare is considered good for 'lower-class' children because it improves their cognitive ability, but not for middle-class children because of the effect of maternal deprivation. █ Another problem that arises is that it is difficult to make comparisons between research findings because studies do not always measure the effects of daycare in the same way. For instance, Shea measures aggressive behaviour while Belsky and Rovine measured attachment differences. █ While both these variables are aspects of social behaviour, they are not comparable. An insecurely attached child may or may not behave aggressively and an aggressive child may or may not be securely attached — thus it is difficult to make valid comparisons. █ McCartney (2004) suggests that whether daycare promotes good developmental outcomes depends on the quality of care. They suggest that individual characteristics, such as temperament, cognitive ability and gender, influence how children experience daycare, and that family variables are better predictors of children's development than are daycare variables, but that high-quality daycare programmes do promote children's intellectual, language and social development. It seems that more research is needed before the question of how daycare affects social development can be reliably answered. █

ⓔ **5–6/6 marks awarded.** In the AO2 section, in █ to █ the student has identified a range of issues and has commented on these issues in depth and in detail using appropriate evidence to support the arguments. There is a clear expression of ideas and the student uses psychological terminology accurately to demonstrate that he or she has a good understanding of the difficulty in drawing any firm conclusions regarding the effect of daycare on children's social development. Another strength of this answer is that, in █ █ █ █ and █ through very effective selection of material it focuses on the question 'as it is set'. Again, most students will struggle to write 300 words of AO2 commentary in 5–6 minutes, but this student has the balance of AO1/AO2 right, which is important in this type of question.

Question 9 **Research methods**

Psychological research suggests that information in STM is acoustically encoded (by sound). In an attempt to test this, 10 participants were asked to read and then recall two lists of 10 words — List A and List B.

The 10 words in List A were: cat, can, cab, tan, bat, ban, fan, fat, hat, pan.

The 10 words in List B were: cot, pig, tap, bet, man, hut, zoo, bee, toe, new.

All the participants first read and then recalled the words in List A, then after a short break they read and then recalled the words in List B.

A table of results is given below.

Participant	Number of words recalled in List A	Number of words recalled in List B
1	4	7
2	3	5
3	5	5
4	3	6
5	2	7
6	5	7
7	7	6
8	5	6
9	4	8
10	3	5

Now answer questions (a)–(f).

(a) Look at the words in each of the lists and explain why the researcher selected those words.   (3 marks)

ⓔ Question injunction = explain. This question assesses AO2 and AO3 skills. One AO2 mark is awarded for your analysis of unfamiliar material in recognising the basis for the selection of words. Two AO3 marks are awarded if you demonstrate your understanding of how and why the IV has been operationalised.

Answers

Student A

The researcher selected the words because all the words in List A sound similar but the words in List B do not sound similar. ⓐ

ⓔ **1/3 marks awarded.** ⓐ Student A has correctly identified the difference between the words in List A and List B but has not explained why this difference was selected.

Student B

The researcher selected the words so that the words in List A are all acoustically similar but the words in List B are not acoustically similar. ⓐ These words were selected because if information in STM is encoded acoustically, the words from List A would be confused and fewer words would be remembered, but the words in List B would not be confused and would be remembered better. ⓑ

ⓔ **3/3 marks awarded — 1 (AO2) mark + 2 (AO3) marks.** ⓐ Student B has correctly identified the difference between the words in List A and List B and ⓑ has then explained why this difference was selected. This answer demonstrates knowledge and understanding of what is being investigated (acoustic encoding in STM) and how this (the DV) was operationalised.

(b) Explain how you could summarise the findings of this investigation. (4 marks)

ⓔ Question injunction = explain. This question assesses AO3 skills and you should show, in detail, your understanding of how data can be summarised. Marks are awarded for:

- description of and justification for the use of appropriate measures of central tendency
- description of and justification for the use of appropriate measures of dispersion
- description of an appropriate graphical display

Answers

Student A

Researchers could calculate and compare the mean and the range of the words remembered in List A and List B conditions ⓐ and draw a scattergram to show the findings. ⓑ

ⓔ **1/4 marks awarded.** Student A's answer is very brief. Although ⓐ the student has suggested a measure of central tendency (the mean), this is not justified as the student has not suggested that the data are ordinal level. The student has suggested that the range be calculated — but has not explained why. The comment ⓑ about 'draw a scattergram' demonstrates a lack of understanding of methodology and data analysis, as the investigation is not a correlational design.

Student B

Researchers could summarise the data in three ways:

(i) Calculate and compare the mean of the words remembered in List A and List B conditions to show whether there is a difference in the measure of central tendency. The mean for List A is 4.1 words and the mean for list B is 6.2 words.

(ii) Because the data are ordinal level, compare the range of words remembered in List A and in List B to show whether there is a difference in measures of dispersion. The range for List A is 5 and the range of List B is 3.

(iii) Draw a visual diagram to depict the data, perhaps a frequency diagram to show the difference in how participants recalled words in each condition, or a bar chart showing the difference in the mean scores in each condition.

Example diagram:

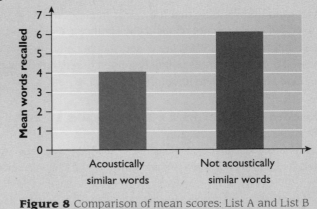

Figure 8 Comparison of mean scores: List A and List B

AQA(A) AS Psychology

ⓔ **4/4 marks awarded.** Student B's answer is very detailed — the student has done a lot of work for 4 marks and has left nothing to chance, having even calculated the mean and the range of both sets of scores. In (i) the answer correctly suggests a measure of central tendency (the mean), but does not justify this by referring to the level of data as ordinal level, but by reference to 'comparison of measures of central tendency'. In (ii) the student has reasonably suggested that the range be calculated — and has justified this by explaining what the range will show. In (iii) the student then continues to suggest two appropriate ways to depict the data graphically and sketches a correctly labelled example. The answer demonstrates knowledge and understanding and is clear and coherent. The strength of this answer lies is its breadth.

(c) Explain what the data appear to show. (4 marks)

ⓔ Question injunction = explain. This question assesses AO3 skills and you must demonstrate that you can interpret the data to explain what the findings of this investigation may mean. Marks are awarded for identification of a difference in performance between the conditions (measures of central tendency in List A and List B) and for explaining why this may have occurred and what it may mean. Marks are also awarded if you identify any differences in the dispersion of the two sets of scores (ranges) and then explain what this may imply.

Answers

Student A

Only four of the ten participants remembered five or more words in List A, but all ten participants remembered five or more words in List B. ⓐ This suggests that List B words were easier to remember than List A words — possibly because they didn't sound the same. ⓑ

ⓔ **1–2/4 marks awarded.** Student A provides a very brief answer, but ⓐ has done 'some work' and ⓑ demonstrates some understanding of the data. The answer gives a basic explanation — 'because the words in List B didn't sound the same' — but this explanation could have been much more clearly expressed.

Student B

The mean number of the List A (acoustically similar) words remembered was 4.1 but the mean number of List B (acoustically dissimilar) words was 6.2. ⓐ This suggests that the acoustic similarity made the words harder to remember than the acoustically dissimilar words and supports the idea that information in STM is coded acoustically. ⓑ However, the range of scores in List A was greater than in List B (List A is 5 while List B is 3). ⓒ This suggests variation in whether the acoustic similarity of words affects how well they are remembered because the same participants took part in both conditions, which excludes participant differences. ⓓ

ⓔ **4/4 marks awarded** Student B gives a clear and detailed answer, demonstrating breadth of understanding of the data and what they may mean. ⓐ The explanation of the difference in the mean scores is coherent and ⓑ is accurately elaborated in terms of the aim of the research. The explanation in ⓒ and ⓓ of the difference in the range of scores is a strength of the answer because the student demonstrates understanding of both the repeated measures design and the research aim. Note that, if the student had given only the explanation of the difference in the mean scores *or* the explanation of the difference in the range of scores, the answer might still have been awarded 4 marks.

(d) Which type of design was used in this investigation: independent measures; repeated measures; or matched participants? (1 mark)

ⓔ Question injunction = 'which type of design was used' implies identify. This question assesses AO3 skills and whether you know the difference between these types of investigation design.

Answers

Student A

Matched participants because the same participants took part in both conditions.

ⓔ **0/1 marks awarded.** Student A gives the wrong answer and demonstrates a common error. Students frequently confuse repeated measures designs with matched participant designs. The student misinterprets the question and wastes time by giving an explanation which is, in any case, incorrect. The answer would be awarded no marks.

Student B

Repeated measures design.

ⓔ **1/1 mark awarded** Student B gives the correct answer.

(e) Identify one weakness in the design of this investigation and explain how the researcher could have overcome this weakness. (3 marks)

ⓔ Question injunction = identify and explain. This question assesses AO3 skills and whether you understand the kinds of problem that psychologists have to overcome when designing research. Your knowledge of the advantages and limitations of independent and repeated measures design and/or sampling methods could be used to answer this question. One mark is awarded for appropriate identification of a weakness of the investigation and 2 marks for explaining how this weakness could be overcome.

Answers

Student A

One weakness of the investigation is there were only ten participants, which is a very small sample, so the results cannot be generalised. To overcome this a larger sample should be used.

ⓔ **0/3 marks awarded.** Student A has not read the question carefully and has not answered the question 'as set'. The question asks for a weakness in the design of the investigation, which requires the answer to refer to the repeated measures design. The answer demonstrates a lack of understanding.

Student B

One weakness of the design of the investigation is in the repeated measures design, in which all the participants remembered List A followed by List B. ⓐ This could lead to 'order effects' because participants might improve with practice, which could explain why participants performed better on List B. ⓑ This weakness could be overcome by having half of the participants remember List A followed by List B and half of the participants remembering List B followed by List A. ⓒ

ⓔ **2–3/3 marks awarded.** Student B's answer is clear and detailed, demonstrating an understanding of one weakness of repeated measures design. The strength of the answer is that ⓐ the student identifies the weakness, ⓑ explains why this is a weakness and then ⓒ gives an appropriate suggestion for how the weakness may be overcome. Although the student does not use the term 'counterbalancing', the answer demonstrates understanding.

(f) Using your knowledge of research methods, discuss the value of laboratory experiments in cognitive psychology.   (4 AO3 marks + 4 AO2 marks)

ⓔ Question injunction = discuss. This question assesses both AO3 and AO2 skills. The key phrases in the question are:

- discuss
- the value of laboratory experiments
- knowledge of research methods

To gain AO3 marks you need to demonstrate your knowledge and understanding of research methods (how science works). You could:

- identify/describe features of the experimental method
- describe how the IV is isolated and manipulated
- describe ways by which the DV is operationalised/measured
- refer to the advantages and disadvantages of collecting quantitative data
- refer to the control of extra variables
- refer to the realism of the procedures

and/or you could:

- use your knowledge of other laboratory experiments (in cognitive psychology), such as studies of memory and of EWT

To gain AO2 marks you need to evaluate the use of laboratory experiments in cognitive psychology. You could refer to:

- the strengths and limitations of laboratory-based experiments
- the usefulness of laboratory-based experiments in increasing understanding of aspects of cognitive psychology (e.g. memory, EWT, improving memory)
- evidence from naturalistic studies that either supports or contradicts the findings of laboratory experiments

Answers

Student A

In a laboratory experiment, researchers try to control all the variables except the independent variable (IV), which is the difference between the experimental conditions. Then the experimenter measures the effect of the IV on the DV, which is what is measured. One advantage of laboratory experiments is that researchers can control other variables that might affect the IV or the DV, thus they can be sure that any effect on the DV is caused by the IV and not by some uncontrolled variable. **a** Also, laboratory experiments can be repeated to check that the findings are reliable. **b**

However, laboratory experiments have low external validity because the procedures used may not measure how people behave outside the laboratory in their everyday lives. **c** For example, when researching memory, participants are often asked to remember lists of words, but people don't often have to remember lists of words in their everyday lives. Also, participants in laboratory experiments know their behaviour is being studied and this can give rise to demand characteristics because participants look for clues in the experiment to tell them how they are expected to behave. **d**

e **2/4 (AO3) and 2–3/4 (AO2)** marks awarded. Student A in **a** to **d** provides a reasonably effective discussion, comprising a brief outline of the main characteristics of laboratory experiments and a reasonably effective evaluation of the methodology. A range of issues, focusing on the strengths and weaknesses of laboratory experiments, is discussed, some in limited depth. Psychological terminology is used accurately and the student demonstrates knowledge and some understanding of research methods. The weakness of the answer is that the student does not address the question of the value of laboratory experiments in an explicit manner, and the answer would be strengthened had the student quoted research evidence to support his or her arguments.

Student B

During a laboratory experiment, researchers try to control all the variables except the independent variable (IV), which is the difference between the experimental conditions. Then the experimenter measures the effect of the IV on the DV, which is what is measured. One advantage of laboratory experiments is that researchers can control extraneous variables that might affect the IV or the DV, thus they can be sure that any effect on the DV is caused by the IV and not by some uncontrolled variable. This is an advantage because statements about cause and effect can be made. **a** In addition, in laboratory experiments control groups can be established, as for example, in the Loftus and Palmer second experiment, where the use of a control group allowed the researchers to be sure that it was the use of the word 'smashed' that caused more participants to report seeing broken glass that wasn't present on the film. **b** This research was valuable because it demonstrated that the way eyewitnesses are questioned can affect the accuracy of their recall. Moreover, controlled laboratory experiments can be repeated to check that the findings are reliable (have not just happened by chance). **c**

However, laboratory experiments have low external validity because the procedures used may not measure how people behave outside the laboratory in their everyday lives. ◾ For example, in the research into how information is encoded in memory (Baddeley), participants were asked to remember lists of words, but people don't often have to remember lists of words in their everyday lives. ◾ That said, it is difficult to see how cognitive psychologists could investigate the encoding of information in memory by naturalistic methods such as by observational studies, and laboratory investigations of encoding, capacity and duration of information in memory have increased our knowledge about human memory. ◾

ⓔ **3–4/4 (AO3) and 4/4 (AO2)** marks awarded. Student B gives a highly effective answer. ◾ The student provides a description of the main characteristics of laboratory experiments and, to demonstrate understanding, ◾ quotes Loftus and Palmer as an accurate example of research in which a control group was established, and why this control group was useful. ◾ The student then explains how the Loftus and Palmer research was useful, which addresses the question of the value of laboratory experiments. In ◾ to ◾ the student continues to identify and discuss a range of issues focusing on the strengths and weaknesses of laboratory experiments, and each issue is explained in reasonable depth. The introduction of ◾ Baddeley in the discussion of external validity is an effective use of material (informed commentary), demonstrating knowledge and understanding. ◾ The final sentence, arguing that human memory cannot be observed, demonstrates knowledge of research methods and again focuses on the question of the value of laboratory experiments. The strength of this answer is the balance of AO3 and AO2 content and the clarity and coherence of the discussion.

1 The capacity for memory is approximately 'seven plus or minus two' pieces of information.

2 STM has limited capacity, approximately seven to nine pieces of information, but LTM has unlimited capacity. Information in STM has limited duration, about 30 seconds, but information in LTM may last a lifetime.

3 The primacy effect occurs because, when a list of information is being memorised, the first items of information are likely to have been transferred to LTM, and the recency effect happens because the last items of information are still in STM.

4 One assumption of the working memory model is that the articulatory–phonological loop has limited capacity. The interference task techniques involve a participant being asked to perform two tasks that use the articulatory–phonological loop, such as reading a book while singing a song. If their performance on both tasks is affected, this is because the articulatory–phonological loop cannot cope with both tasks.

5 The study by Loftus and Palmer was a laboratory experiment but Yuille and Cutshall was an experimental case study. The participants in Loftus and Palmer were students, but Yuille and Cutshall participants had witnessed a violent crime.

6 In a cognitive interview the police take care to reduce the anxiety felt by witnesses. They minimise distractions, avoid interruptions and allow the witness to take his or her time. The witness is encouraged to report every tiny detail of the event, recreate the context of the event, recall the event in different orders, and may be asked to recall the event imagining what someone in a different place might have seen. Recreating the context and imagining the event from a different perspective may provide contextual cues that help the witness remember the event.

7 Jane may remember more as information that is organised is more likely to be remembered, because each remembered fact will activate other related information. As Jane thinks about each fact this will activate and consolidate previously existing memory, increasing the likelihood that she will remember the learned information.

8 A child's bond with his or her caregiver can be explained in terms of learning and reinforcement, because the caregiver relieves the physical needs of hunger and thirst and the child learns to associate pleasure with the caregiver.

9 According to Bowlby, infants have an innate tendency to form an attachment and attachment takes place during a critical period or not at all.

10 A securely attached infant shows some anxiety when the caregiver departs but is easily soothed, plays independently and greets the caregiver's return with enthusiasm. In insecure–avoidant attachment, the infant shows indifference when the caregiver leaves and at reunion the infant actively avoids contact with the caregiver. In insecure–resistant attachment the infant is distressed when the caregiver goes but, when the caregiver returns, the infant may resist contact and is not easily consoled.

11 Maternal privation is when a child has never been able to develop an attachment to his or her mother or another caregiver.

12 Adoptive parents put a lot of effort into relationships between themselves and their children but do not make special efforts to ensure good relationships between their children and peers.

13 A positive correlation was found, because as time spent in daycare increased so did the rating for aggression.

14 Shea concluded that daycare has a positive effect on peer relationships. Two groups of children aged between 3 and 4 years were studied. One group attended nursery school for five days a week and the other group attended twice a week. During their first 10 weeks of attending nursery school, the children were assessed and both groups increased their social skills, were less aggressive and interacted more with others.

15 In high quality daycare (a) the staff are trained; (b) there is an appropriate ratio of staff to children; (c) low staff turnover allows children to form stable attachments with carers; (d) age-appropriate toys and activities are provided.

16 This is a laboratory experiment because it was conducted in a controlled and artificial setting. The variable that changed was the position of the words in the list. The DV was how frequently each of the words was remembered.

17 This is a natural experiment because the IV, whether the child attended a day nursery or a childminder, is naturally occurring and the children could not be randomly allocated to these conditions.

18 Sharing a toy, playing a game with another child, giving a toy to another child, comforting another child.

19 Examples:
(a) Is your child happy to share toys with other children? YES or NO
(b) Does your child ever behave aggressively with other children? YES or NO
(c) Which of these best describes your child? My child behaves aggressively — Very often; Often, Rarely, Never

20 Example answers: Participant confidentiality — participants should not be asked to provide names and addresses or details that could identify them. Informed consent — participants should be told the true purpose of the research. Protection — participants should not be asked embarrassing questions.

21 Participants who are asked to estimate the speed of the cars when they *smashed* into each other will be significantly more likely to report seeing broken glass than participants who are asked to estimate the speed of the cars when they *hit* each other.

22 There is no significant difference in the speed reported by participants who are asked to estimate how fast the cars are travelling whether they are asked a question containing the word *contacted, bumped, collided, hit* or *smashed.*

23 Texting; using the phone as a camera; using the phone to listen to music; talking on the phone.

24 An opportunity sample is biased because it will probably comprise friends of the researcher, or students, and the people approached will be those who are local and available — thus all the participants are likely to have similar characteristics.

25 This question might give rise to social desirability bias because parents would want to show their child in the most positive manner. So, when answering this question, they might give answers that underestimate their child's aggressive behaviour.

26 In a small sample of scores the mean can be distorted by extremely high or low scores in the data set.

27 Measures of central tendency tell us the average value of a set of scores, but measures of dispersion tell us about how 'spread out' the scores are.

28 Possible categories: (a) pushing; (b) fighting; (c) arguing; (d) swearing; (e) hitting.